A
Table
for Two

A Table for Two

*A mother and her young daughter
face death together . . .*

Alisa Bair

Good Books

Intercourse, PA 17534

Design by Dawn J. Ranck
Cover illustration by Cheryl Benner

A TABLE FOR TWO
Copyright © 1998 by Good Books
Good Books, Intercourse, PA 17534
International Standard Book Number: 1-56148-218-8
Library of Congress Catalog Card Number: 97-50193

Library of Congress Cataloging-in-Publication Data
Bair, Alisa.
    A table for two : a mother and her young daughter face death together-- / Alisa
Bair.
        p. cm.
    Includes bibliographical references.
    ISBN 1-56148-218-8
    1. Bair, Kelly. 2. Christian biography--United States. 3. Intracranial tumors in
children--Patients--United States--Biography. 4. Bair, Alisa. 5. Intracranial tumors in
children--Patients--Family relationships. 6. Grief--Religious aspects--Christianity.
7. Children--Death--Religious aspects--Christianity.
I. Title
BR1725.B3313B35   1998
248.8'66'092
[B]--DC21   97-50193
                                                                                CIP

"Thou preparest a table before me in
the presence of mine enemies. . . ."
— Psalm 23:5 (KJV)

For all who have not yet tasted . . .

1.

Dr. Warren led me into the hospital conference room and closed the door. Lowering myself into a chair, I anxiously searched his face for a clue of what he was about to tell me. Something in his manner had already carried a message, and my heart beat heavily in response.

Sitting down beside me, he looked at me sympathetically for a moment. "I wish I had good news," he started, his breath suspended ominously between us, close enough to feel it on my face. "But I don't."

His words siphoned the blood out of me. A searing heat coursed through my veins and burned me into the chair.

"We found the cause of Kelly's vomiting. She has a lesion at the base of her brain. The good news is that it's accessible."

"Lesion? Accessible?" I floundered to understand.

"A mass. Fortunately it's located where we can operate." He pulled an X-ray-like picture out of an envelope and pointed to a shadowy section at the back of her head, just above her neck. "The MRI shows the mass up against the brain stem, but we won't know until we operate whether or not it's attached. It's critical that the brain stem not be touched in surgery."

Like a tidal wave, Dr. Warren's words crashed against my heart. He paused, searching my face for damage. I groped for my bearings, not fully trusting what I had just heard. "Could you please call my husband at home and explain all this to him?" It was 7:30 a.m. Rob would not yet have left for work.

I stood up, and willed my body forward and out the door. *Dear God! What will I tell Kelly? How can a six-year-old deal with this? Help me!* Rounding the corner into the hall, I sensed that the activity at the nurses' station froze as I passed. They stood quietly, their eyes following me respectfully. *They all know,* I thought.

I walked into Kelly's room, sat down in the chair beside her bed, and fixed my eyes on the TV where Bert and Ernie were chatting obliviously.

"Mommy, what did he say?" Kelly asked, her thin, weak voice heightening my heartache.

I snapped off the TV, moved to her bed, and curled my body around her. Stroking her legs, I searched for the right words, held back my tears.

"They found out what's making you so sick." I paused; her blue eyes gazed intently at me. "There's something called a 'lesion' in your brain. It's pressing on a nerve, and that makes you feel like vomiting."

Her eyes widened with concern. I wrestled with how to continue and proceeded as gently as I could. "They have to operate to take it out, or you won't get better."

At these words, Kelly burst into tears. "I don't want to have surgery," she sobbed. Her cry of fear shattered my fragile exterior. Helplessly, I lay my head on her heaving chest and cried with her. She held me in her arms, and then her concern for me overrode her own fears. "M-m-mommy," she stammered. "Why are you crying?"

"I hurt when you hurt," I said as simply and honestly as I could, without letting her know the full weight of my agony. "Jesus," I prayed weakly. "Please help us . . ."

On a morning three weeks earlier, I awakened to the sound of Kelly getting sick in the bathroom. *Again,* I thought in puzzled frustration as I made my way down the stairs and into the kitchen. Pulling the calendar off the refrigerator, I tried to recall the intermittent dates in the previous five weeks that had begun the same way. I circled them, startled to see this was the seventh.

"Mom, Kelly got sick again," our 14-year-old daughter Lauren stated as she came into the kitchen for breakfast.

"I know, I heard her."

"Are you sure we can't catch what she has?"

"Well, if you could catch it, you'd have caught it by now," I answered. "This isn't acting like a virus. But I honestly don't know what it is."

The pattern was always the same: After vomiting once upon waking, Kelly would lie in bed for a while longer, then perk up and get ready for school, barely catching the bus behind Leslie, her 11-year-old sister. "Are you sure you feel well enough to go?" I'd ask. The answer was always yes. The nausea never lingered, and there were never accompanying symptoms. The first few times, with five or seven days between episodes, I thought little of it.

"If I didn't know better," I joked with a friend, "I'd think she had morning sickness!" But I was beginning to carry a nagging concern. And when the school nurse called me the morning I circled the dates, saying Kelly had vomited during class, I decided it was time to consult the doctor.

When Rob brought her home from her appointment that afternoon, I smiled with relief as I helped her take her medicine. "Aren't you glad we finally found the reason for this?" Coincidentally, she had registered a low-grade fever and presented a red throat with some sinus drainage. No other symptoms present, the doctor surmised she had a chronic sinus infection which was draining during the night and causing an acidic, upset stomach in the morning.

For five days she didn't vomit at all, and we were worry-free—until the next day when she vomited twice, then continued to do the same for three more consecutive mornings.

Another doctor in the practice switched her to a different type of antibiotic, but the morning after her first two doses, she vomited six times. "Stop the antibiotic," he told me over the phone. "We're barking up the wrong tree here. Bring her in first thing tomorrow morning."

The next day, after Kelly's exam showed no problems, the doctor fished the same pond the others had. "No headaches? Dizziness? Nothing that might be upsetting her emotionally?" He looked at me thoughtfully. If he suspected anything more serious, he graciously spared me. "I'd like to schedule an upper gastrointestinal scan. It's not unheard of for children to have stomach ulcers."

The morning of the scan, four days later, was not pleasant. By the time we arrived at the diagnostic imaging center, Kelly had already gotten sick twice. "I hope she can keep the barium down," I told the technician. Wondrously, she was able to drink the chalky liquid and contain it during the exam, even as the machine gently rocked her into various positions. Conveniently, the barium came back up only moments following, just as the technician was outlining drinking instructions for moving it out of Kelly's system. My heart ached for all I was putting this young child through, but I was hopeful that we would now find the reason for all this. "Mommy, is that the last test I have to have?" Kelly asked as we drove home, her head resting in a pillow propped against the window, legs pulled up onto the seat.

"I think so, honey," I said, laying my hand on her knee and rubbing it gently. "Not the best way to end your first-grade year, is it?"

It was the tenth of June. The 1991-92 school term had closed only two days before, and it brought changes for all of us. Lauren finished eighth grade and Leslie fifth. Although Kelly missed the last few days of school, she completed all her work. Rob ended another year as counselor to the high school freshman class and would soon begin his summer work on the district maintenance crew.

Perking up by afternoon, Kelly drank some fluids, ate a decent supper, and did not get sick at all the next day. But the day following, the vomiting resumed, and her nausea continued—this time into the late afternoon and on into the night.

The next morning, the doctor reported no abnormalities from the scan. He scheduled a blood test for the following day, but by that evening, I noticed Kelly's shorts hanging loosely around her waist. After helping her upstairs and onto the bathroom scale, I was shocked to see she had dropped eight pounds. Up to this point the doctors and we had moved patiently through the logical steps of diagnostic procedure. Suddenly I didn't feel patient or logical anymore.

I went immediately to the phone, hoping to catch a doctor at the health center before closing time. "It's just so hard," I told the receptionist tearfully, "not knowing what's causing this." She summoned Dr. Warren, with whom we had originally consulted, to the phone. Since he hadn't handled her case or seen Kelly recently, I had to update him. "You can go ahead and rule out any psychological cause for this," I said, impatient with his newness in the practice and subsequent unfamiliarity with us as patients. "Something's wrong. She's now vomiting round-the-clock, and I just weighed her and found that she's lost eight pounds."

"Bring her in at noon tomorrow," he said, his voice decidedly less nonchalant. "By then we'll have the results of her blood work. We may have to hospitalize her for intractable vomiting."

By noon the following day Kelly was severely weakened. Any change in position made her sick. With Rob at work and Lauren and Leslie away at track and gymnastic practices, I dressed her and carried her to the backseat of the car where, after we arrived at the doctor's office, she lay unmoving.

"I can't go in," she pleaded. "Please don't move me." We waited for a few moments until she vomited again, and then I carried her in.

"Kelly's blood test is normal," Dr. Warren stated thoughtfully as he examined her. "But I'd like to hospitalize her. We can do more tests in there. I'll call and tell them you're coming. She's not dehydrated, but she is dry."

Slowly, gingerly, I carried her back to the car. I had mentioned to Rob that hospitalization was a possibility, and I had arranged for the girls' transportation home from their sports practices, just in case. But I was so focused on getting Kelly into the hospital and onto intravenous fluids, that I didn't bother to stop at home for extra clothing, or think to ask somebody to ride with us.

Twenty minutes later, parked on the street in front of the hospital, I scooped Kelly up into my arms and over my shoulder, plastic dish in hand, and made my way across traffic. Pausing frequently on the sidewalk for her to hover over the dish, I regretted my lack of foresight in not getting someone else to drive and drop us off at the entrance.

Entering at the lower level, we slowly made our way through a tunnel-like passageway. We stopped several times so Kelly could drop her head to her knees. Finally, someone offered to get her a wheelchair. I gratefully accepted.

On the pediatric unit, two doctors put Kelly through a series of neurological tests. "Kelly, can you walk along this line here?"

"Now can you shut your eyes and do it?"

"Keep your head straight and follow my finger with your eyes. . . ." To my untrained view, Kelly appeared to exhibit nothing unusual.

"Don't worry, Mrs. Bair," one of them said. "We'll get to the root of this."

Because her undiagnosed illness was possibly contagious, we were directed to a private room. I was grateful to discover I could sleep on a cot beside her during the night. Helping Kelly into bed, I tried to reassure both of us. "Pretty soon they'll get you hooked up to an IV, and you should start to feel a little better."

"Are they going to stick me?"

"Yes, they have to, but it'll be quick. Then, after that, they can give you all your medicine through it, and they won't have to stick you again."

Once she was hooked up to IV fluids, I called Rob to tell him that we had indeed come into the hospital. After work, he arrived along with Lauren and Leslie. They cheered the room like fresh flowers, but Kelly was too sick to even smile at them.

Rob brought Kelly's worn, pink teddy—rescued from the closet shelf where she had relegated him the year before when she tried to stop sucking her thumb. In fact, she had told us to hide him from her.

"Ted wanted desperately to be with you," Rob said gently, holding him out in front of her and tilting the now-floppy bear's head.

"I just couldn't stay away, knowing you were so sick," came his tiny, treble, cartoon voice. His paws nudged her arm. "Is it okay if I stay?" Kelly managed a faint smile as she lifted the corner of her sheet and welcomed this beloved friend once again. Rob tucked him under her arm, then pulled up the sheets until only their heads protruded from the top.

"Mrs. Bair?" a voice interrupted. I turned to face the pediatric resident standing in the doorway.

"We've scheduled Kelly for an MRI this evening. Transport will be by to pick her up around 5:45." He smiled cordially. "We're right here if you need us for anything."

An MRI. Another procedure. Each time I prepared Kelly for a needle prick or a test, I hoped it would be the last. What would I tell her about magnetic resonance imaging? That I knew adults who dreaded it, felt claustrophobic, and hated it? And what about her vomiting? I knew you had to lie still in a constrictive, tunnel-like opening while pictures were taken and a noise like a jackhammer sounded in your ears.

My heart went out to this dear child as I stroked her forehead and smoothed back her soft, blonde hair. Robust and vivacious only weeks before, she looked weak and delicate now. The loss of weight and fluid made her features more defined, and her face, usually brimming with mischief and a feisty zest for living, was sickly still. Her long eyelashes lay softly on her cheekbones and seemed to melt into her now sallow complexion.

"Kelly?" I said. Her lashes parted and batted sleepily. "After a little while we have to go downstairs for a test called an MRI."

"Will it hurt?"

"I don't think so. But you have to be very still while they take pictures of your head. I'll stay with you the whole time, okay?"

Rob and I shared an early supper in the cafeteria while Lauren and Leslie stayed with Kelly. Afterwards, transport arrived. Threading our way down floors and through countless halls and right angles, we finally arrived in the radiology department. "She's extremely nauseated," I told the technician who greeted us. "What if she vomits during this?"

Summoning a nurse who administered a suppository, our technician instructed me to remove all metal objects from my person. She guided us into a small room where Kelly was shifted onto a narrow bed which extended out from the circular opening of what looked like a giant clothes dryer. Thankfully, she was allowed to keep her teddy with her.

Suppressing all my anxiety, I talked to Kelly constantly, soothing her and repeating the technician's instructions. After locking her head into a frame and covering her with a blanket, the woman handed her a rubber bulb connected to a long tube. "If you want me to stop for any reason, or if you want to come out, just squeeze this, okay? I'll talk to you while you're in there. What music do you like? Do you have a favorite radio station I can play for you?"

Kelly was too sick to respond or exhibit any anxiety she might have felt. I chose the station for her, the technician pushed a button, and Kelly was powered into the opening of the machine. Leaving the room, the woman took her place like an airplane pilot behind a set of controls which I could see through a glass window. I had promised Kelly I would assure her I was nearby by touching her feet. I squeezed her toes. "I'll touch your feet again after the picture's over," I said. "Right now I'm going to sit in a chair beside you."

"Kelly, this first picture is for 10 minutes," came the voice of the technician over the speaker. "Are you okay?"

"Yes," came her faint response from inside the machine. There was a loud groan, and then the jackhammer noise began, just like it had been described to me. It continued relentlessly for 10 minutes. And then it was over.

"How was that, Kelly? Are you okay? Good. This next picture is for 15 minutes. Now stay real still. You're doing great."

Halfway through, the technician returned to us and powered Kelly out of the tunnel for a short time while she injected dye into Kelly's IV.

"You're doing super, sweetie," I said. The whole event hadn't appeared to faze her.

One hour later, she was finished. Relieved, we returned to our room. Kelly smiled briefly as Lauren and Leslie handed her a balloon and some tiny gifts. After visiting a while longer, we held hands and prayed together before exchanging good-bye hugs and kisses.

Tucked in for the night, I listened to the IV machine gurgling softly beside us in the darkened room. The sound reminded me of a rotating fan we had at home. I relaxed, relieved that we were under the care of doctors and nurses. And I tried to prepare myself for what I knew would be a long night of medical interruptions.

My mind traveled through the events of the day and lingered on my husband's comment after dinner, which he made as we stood outside the hospital, taking in some fresh air. Somebody at work suggested to him that vomiting can sometimes be caused by a brain tumor. Rob had a tendency to jump to catastrophic conclusions about the slightest symptom, so I chuckled to get him to stop worrying. Surely it couldn't be something *that* serious.

Now, in the darkness where fears enlarge, I imagined a

A TABLE FOR TWO

sober-faced doctor knocking on the door in the morning with bad news: *Mrs. Bair, would you mind stepping out into the hall, please* . . .

2.

The morning after Kelly was admitted to the hospital dawned bright and sunny. I dressed, put away my cot, and turned on the TV so she could watch her morning shows. Daylight put my fears to rest, and so when Dr. Warren knocked on the door, entering with a smile and a cheery greeting for Kelly, I was relaxed and glad to see him.

"Kelly," he said, still smiling, "I need to talk with your mother down the hall for a few minutes. I'll bring her back soon, okay?"

The smile he turned on so brightly for her snapped off like a light when we stepped out of her line of vision. We walked together in silence to the conference room.

Now, my head swirling with the information he had given, I pressed my face to Kelly's chest, our tears intermingling. My worst imaginings had come true. The thought of surgery loomed monstrously before Kelly. We had prayed for help. Desperately, I pondered what to do next. I was a body groping in quicksand.

We didn't have long to cry. Dr. Warren returned, saying he had reached Rob and that he was on his way. Surgery would be in two days, he reported. Sensitive to our need to be alone, he left the room.

"Mommy, w-will I wake up in surgery?" Kelly asked, drawing in a breath punctuated by sobs.

"No, honey," I said, reaching for a Kleenex and wiping my nose. "You won't feel a thing."

"Would I feel it if they pricked my toe with a pin?"

"Nope."

"Would I feel it if they pinched me real hard?"

"Nope."

"How 'bout if they hit me with a hammer?"

"Absolutely not."

Her face relaxed considerably. "Okay, I trust you," she sighed. I smiled, comforted slightly by having allayed her fears even a little.

Suddenly the door swung open, and the calm we had begun to foster in our conversation was disrupted by the abrupt greeting of a gray-haired man who stood in cool precision before us. He introduced himself as the neurosurgeon who, in the emergency absence of the pediatric neurosurgeon, would perform Kelly's surgery. His voice, strong and matter-of-fact, cut through the air like a steel blade.

"Well, I guess you know it's a brain tumor."

His words startled me. We had been calling it a lesion. I'd known—but had I really?

A *brain tumor.* The words were weighty, but it was a common term I now clearly understood. While gentle Dr. Warren used correct medical jargon to give me a clear indication of the severity of Kelly's condition, his words had cushioned the blow. This doctor, however, was all business.

My mind numbly absorbed his description of three common brain tumor types occurring in children of Kelly's age—two cancerous; one not. He moved to the bed, asked Kelly to sit up, and proceeded to do a number of tests. I ached for her, sick as she was. Finally he asked her to sit on the edge of the bed and look up at the ceiling. This simple position, pinching the area at the back of her neck where the tumor was located, made her whole body shudder. I was in agony. In one swift blow, the medical community had nailed her case, and the harsh reality crushed me.

He confirmed the surgery for Saturday morning, two days away, and left the room. When he was gone, Kelly's eyes met mine. "I don't want to have surgery," she said again, her eyes refilling with tears. Her quivering chin disarmed the little control I had, and I moved to her bed and snuggled close to her. She cried hard, and it occurred to me that six-year-olds need to let it out, too.

When her tears slowed a little, she asked why I was crying. What could I tell her? How scared I was? How thoughts about life and death were swirling so mightily within me that I could scarcely bear the weight of my own body? I yearned to be in control for her sake. But I was helplessly out of control. I glanced at the apple I took off the parents' breakfast cart an hour earlier. I couldn't imagine ever being hungry again.

Rob and the girls arrived as soon as they could. And by afternoon, Kelly received a refreshing splash of visitors. In combination with the IV fluids and medication to reduce the swelling around the tumor, these friends began to perk up Kelly. Balloons, stuffed animals, flowers, and kids decorated the room and lightened our hearts.

Occasionally Rob and I left the room to talk or make a phone call out of Kelly's hearing. Often I went with a friend to the empty conference room, where I shed my parental role and cried like the scared child I was. These friends shouldered my pain and my fear. It was as if they sponged up my seeping heart with great towels of compassion and mercy. When one particular spasm of emotion ended, I returned to Kelly, surprised to find her giggling.

"We were discussing how adorable Kelly will look in her new haircut after surgery," said one friend. Kelly laughed heartily as she swept her hair up and modeled various hairdos. *Dear God,* I thought. *Where does this resilience come from?* Deeply grateful, I found my own spirits lifting in response to her giggles.

But in the middle of all this cheer came the voices of family and friends, jaywalking through Rob's and my emotional traffic:

"You need to find the best pediatric neurosurgeon available."

"I heard there's an excellent one in Pittsburgh."

"I've heard Boston is excellent."

"Johns Hopkins has a terrific reputation."

"You'll benefit by being close by; my doctor said he would send his child to Hershey."

"My friend who's a nurse says Children's Hospital of Philadelphia is the best."

The advice, while coming from the mouths of well-loved and well-intentioned people, enlarged our turmoil. One doctor friend had great accolades for the neurosurgeon scheduled to operate on Kelly. "But if it were my child, I'd really want to find someone experienced in pediatric neurosurgery."

We never had to deal with these kinds of decisions before, let alone all the emotion that accompanied them. By evening, I was confused and fatigued. I said good-bye to Kelly and Rob, who would stay the night with her, and went with Lauren and Leslie down the hall.

Waiting for the elevator, I happened to mention the words "brain tumor" in our conversation. Leslie gasped. "Mom, you mean Kelly has a *brain tumor?*" Her eyes widened with fear. "I thought it was a lesion." She began to cry. "Is she—going to die?"

Lauren's eyes filled, too. I embraced them both. "Right now we need to focus on Kelly's operation. I don't know what's ahead for her. Only God knows, and trusting Him is all we can do."

We reached the hospital lobby and saw Rob's sister Linda and her husband coming toward us. I had tried unsuccessfully to reach her all day. She smiled broadly at seeing us, but her face sobered instantly as I told her the diagnosis. She hugged us hard, promising she'd be cheerful for Kelly. But as we exited through the automatic doors, I saw her detour into the sitting area and put her head in her hands.

The girls and I arrived home to greet Tucker, our one-year-old miniature collie. Wriggling and squealing in his crate, he bounded out and attacked us with kisses. The phone rang: "Lisa, is it true . . . ?"

And again: "I heard today that . . . "

The calls came in a steady stream. Finally, they tailed off. "Girls," I said, "let's get to bed. We need some good sleep. These are going to be long days ahead."

I crawled into bed, my mind reeling, my body registering the trauma. Feeling feverish, I took a pair of Tylenol to settle the trembling. My prayers for strength and wisdom went up in a wordless heap. Deep, agonizing, silent groans echoed from the walls of my soul.

When I awoke the next morning it was all still there, heavy and ominous. Depressed, I gathered clean clothes and toiletries and drove to the hospital. I wearily turned down the hall to Kelly's room, expecting to link up with an even sicker child and a husband as depressed as I.

Entering her doorway, I stopped in my tracks to take in the scene. Kelly, propped up in a sitting position, nibbled at an English muffin and a platter of scrambled eggs. Rob's folded cot held a neat stack of sheets and blankets. Balloons and stuffed animals were lined up in rows. My wonderful husband had brought his gift of order to the room. They both smiled a greeting. My mouth fell open. "Kelly, you're *eating.*"

"Good news, Mom," Rob said for both of them. Kelly smiled and looked at Rob as if they held a special secret. "The medicine reduced the swelling and improved her enough so that we can take a little more time to decide where she should go for surgery." His words and their smiles lightened my heart.

"Mommy, is today your birthday?"

Kelly's words jolted me. "Uh, yes, I guess it is." A birthday had never seemed so irrelevant. She flashed Rob a look as if to say, *See, I told you, and we don't even have any presents.*

"We'll celebrate another time," I assured her. "Right now, all that's important is getting you better."

"Mommy, when Aunt Lin was here last night, she promised me a pizza party today," Kelly said with a grin.

"A pizza party?" I laughed to myself, enjoying the fantasy. Linda *had* managed to be cheerful.

While the morning smorgasbord of children's TV shows entertained Kelly, Rob and I talked at length about what to do. He met the doctor in charge of follow-up treatment who, regrettably, would be on vacation the next week. Gradually I began to absorb the reality that surgery was not going to end this ordeal. Not only did we have to decide on the right hospital in which to have surgery, but we also needed to consider— in the event the tumor was malignant—where to go for long-term, specialized, pediatric treatment, which our local hospital did not provide.

Cancer. The probability had registered only slightly with me. In spite of the neurosurgeon's speculation that Kelly's tumor was not the benign type, I simply could not absorb the potential reality of it. The fact of my daughter's brain being touched in surgery was large and unsettling. I could think beyond it to nothing else—except, perhaps, the possibility of death. . . .

As I had been doing off and on for a solid week now, I replayed a picture that came into my mind one day when Kelly was one year old. Out of the blue it had come, a peaceful scene of her as an older child, perhaps seven or eight, lying still like a porcelain doll in a white bed of some sort, with white, bar-like lines around it. I knew it was she because of the blonde hair—distinctive in our family of brunettes—and I knew she was dead.

It wasn't a horrible picture, and, though it was mildly disturbing, I wasn't frightened by it. It wasn't one of those fearful images that can flash through the minds of protective mothers raising their vulnerable children in a precarious world. I knew those kinds of images; I'd had plenty with all my daughters. This was different.

Still, I never spoke it out loud to Rob, not even when he wanted to paint Kelly's brown, wooden crib white. Some things are just too deep and mysterious, and there remains the fear that talking about them will bring them to reality. "She'll be out of it before you know it," I'd said. "Let's not bother."

The white bar-like lines . . . were they crib bars? *Lord God, what did the vision mean?*

A knock on the door interrupted my reverie. A Domino's Pizza delivery man? In a hospital?

"Kelly Bair?" he asked, checking his slip.

"Yes," I responded for her incredulously, taking the pizza box he offered me.

"It's already paid for," he said. "Have a good day."

I opened the box to reveal one big slice of pizza and a note: "Dear Kelly, A deal's a deal. Enjoy! Love, Aunt Lin."

3.

One by one, friends and family poured into Kelly's room after lunch until, at one point, I counted 15 people surrounding her bed. While Kelly appeared to be enormously buoyed by their presence and the array of gifts coming her direction, I was overwhelmed. The unresolved decisions, compounded by all the commotion, rode like out-of-control rafts over the white water of my emotions.

Slipping into a vacant room across the hall, I leaned on the frame of some bunk beds for support. Rob, also looking for a quiet place, soon joined me. We were riding a swift, downstream current, heading for a spill into deep waters unfamiliar even to our parents. Who could counsel us but God? Rob gathered me close to his side and prayed out loud for wisdom.

Help was immediately forthcoming. "There you are! I've been looking for you," said the doctor in charge of oncology follow-up protocol, popping his head inside the door. His manner was warm and affable, and he knew our dilemma. "In light of your wishes, the unavailability of our pediatric neurosurgeon, and my absence next week, if it's okay with you, I've set up a consultation for you with Dr. Leslie Sutton at Children's Hospital of Philadelphia [CHOP] tomorrow."

The burden lifted dramatically. Not only had he chosen the

hospital we were leaning toward, but he had also set up all the connections. We had felt subversive, even underhanded, in choosing not to go with the neurosurgeon assigned to us. Instead of dropping us like we imagined, the hospital supported us. We were inexpressibly grateful.

"Your township ambulance will transport Kelly in the morning," he said, smiling sympathetically and extending his hand to each of us. "The best of luck to you."

Across the hall, I spotted our pastor arriving at Kelly's door. We'd only attended his church for four months, so we were really just beginning to know him, but already there was a kindred spirit between us. He had stopped to check on us several hours before, and now he was back at our request to perform a service of anointing.

"Kelly," I said, returning to her bedside after saying good-bye to most of the visitors. "Pastor Tom has come to pray with us and anoint you, like it says in the Bible to do when somebody's sick."

"What's 'anoint' mean?" she asked as she examined a small game someone had given her.

"It means he's going to put a little oil on your forehead, and we're all going to pray. I've been anointed before, and it's just a way of asking God to heal you. Is that all right with you?" She nodded.

We gathered the remaining family members around Kelly's bed. Taking a little bottle of oil from his pocket, Pastor Tom opened his Bible to the book of James and began to read: ". . . Is any one of you sick? He should call the elders of the church to pray over him and anoint him with oil in the name of the Lord. And the prayer offered in faith will make the sick person well; the Lord will raise him up . . . "

He held his finger over the opening, turned the bottle upside down, and moistened his finger with oil. "Kelly," he said, tenderly making the sign of the cross on her forehead. "I anoint you in the name of the Father, the Son, and the Holy Spirit." Then he placed his other hand on her head. "Please join with me in prayer as the Spirit leads."

Kneeling, standing, or crouching, each with a hand on her body, we offered her to God. Prayers, brief but heartfelt, rose like incense around the room. I opened my eyes to take in the scene. My daughters and nieces, deeply sobered by their young comrade's infirmity, prayed silently. My sister Abby, tears reddening her face, offered her heart's cry. Rob, stroking Kelly's blanketed feet, prayed all he could pray in the moment. "Protect her, Lord," he said, his voice choking. These were simple, intense prayers. All we could do was touch her and present our bleeding, hoping hearts to God.

I closed my eyes, and suddenly there was the scene of Kelly in the white bed again. Only now she was leaping out of it, her blonde hair flying, her voice full of laughter. Did it mean healing, or did it mean heaven? God, in his mercy, would not tell me. *I have much more to say to you,* Jesus told His disciples after He began to prepare them for His own death—*more than you can now bear . . .*

An atmosphere of hope filled the room as we broke away from our prayer circle. Before anyone could leave, my mother stopped us. "Wait just a minute," she said, taking a paper sack off her chair and pulling out an assortment of chocolate whoopie pies. "We have a birthday here today, and—" she eyed me compassionately, "while this isn't much, we can't let the day go by without at least acknowledging it." It was the gesture of a mother's heart, ever mindful of her daughter, and a celebration appropriately tempered by our circumstances.

After almost everyone had gone, a close friend appeared in our doorway. "Have you had it with visitors?" she said shyly, smiling apologetically.

"Beth! Come in," I said, hugging her.

She sat down beside Kelly's bed and handed me a large, beautifully wrapped box. "Here, this is for Kelly—and for your birthday." Overwhelmed by her thoughtfulness, I slowly unwrapped the tissue paper. Inside was a framed drawing of Jesus tenderly holding a lamb to his face. His eyes closed, his nose buried in the soft fleece, it was a picture I knew well—a work of art emanating holy tenderness and mercy. I had gotten it for two different friends at crisis points in their lives and had wanted one for myself, but I couldn't locate another.

"Where did you find this?" I said, elated to finally have one in my possession. The scene has a quality of restoration, and it began to melt me deeply as I looked at it. Beth watched me silently and tenderly, her dark eyes full of compassion. Then I remembered she had received the picture at Christmas and had hung it on the wall of her baby's nursery. "This is *your* picture," I said, suddenly comprehending, my eyes filling. "I can't accept this—"

"Yes you can; you need it the most right now. I want you to have it. I'll find another one sometime." It was a sacrificial gift, bestowed in the spirit of two childhood friends entrusting their most beloved possession—like a very piece of their hearts—into the safekeeping of the other.

"Mrs. Bair," came a nurse's voice in the doorway. "The ambulance will arrive at 6:00 tomorrow morning, an hour earlier than you were told. Also, CHOP has requested another MRI, this time of Kelly's spine. I'm afraid we can't get her in for that until 9:00 tonight."

Quickly, the anxiety returned. Beth sensed it. "Lisa, I spoke to Jeff and Donna. They live 20 minutes from CHOP, and they'd be happy to have you stay with them, if you need a place."

Later, when I discovered no rooms were available at the Ronald McDonald House, I dialed their number, thankful to have these friends, our only acquaintances in the Philadelphia area, to fall back on. Donna's soothing voice calmed me.

"I don't know what to expect," I said, "but we'll let you know if we need your place after we talk to the neurosurgeon."

Like a team preparing for a big game, our family huddled around Kelly and planned strategy: "We'll need to get up at 4:45 a.m."

"Four forty-five? Ugh. . . "

"Les, I'm showering first . . ."

"Rob, please make sure you do a load of whites, and don't forget to pack my sneakers and Kelly's nightie . . . "

"Les, please make sure Tucker gets some exercise tomorrow morning . . . "

"Who's taking care of him when we go?"

"Lauren, don't forget to call Dwight and Carol. I couldn't reach them . . ."

Finally we huddled for prayer. Then, laden with flowers, balloons, and stuffed animals, they were gone. Kelly and I looked mournfully at each other. Stripped of all that had filled it, our room lost its smile. We turned on the TV to escape the loneliness and wearily waited for our MRI transport.

It was 10:00 when they finally came. Veterans now, we endured the scan easily. At 11:15 we arrived back up on our floor, the IV pole—affectionately named "Sally" by Pastor Tom—bumping along beside us.

"Mommy, could I have an apple cut into pieces?"

Anxious to meet the needs of this sick little girl, particularly to feed her, I swung into action to find one. I had finally eaten mine earlier, so I checked the snack room, then asked a nurse if there were any on the floor. Ten minutes later, a nurse appeared in the doorway with an apple. "The kitchen was closed, but we were able to find you one," she said.

I smiled, thanked her, and turned toward Kelly, but she had already fallen asleep. I brushed her forehead lightly with my lips, then dressed for bed and climbed into my cot. Pulling the covers over me, my thoughts slipped back to the last time we were in the hospital together, almost seven years before . . .

4.

"You have a little girl," the doctor announced at 9:45 a.m. on Tuesday, July 30th, 1985. I lifted my head to see this new baby, our third daughter. Her hair was still wet, but unmistakably blonde, a real contrast to both Rob and me and also to Lauren and Leslie, who both had thick, dark hair at birth.

I took the swaddled bundle from the nurse and placed her at my breast, where she began to suck tentatively. Rob and I studied her intently, eager to know her and determine whether our chosen name for her, "Kelly Marie," would match her sweet form.

When we came home from the hospital a few days later, Kelly's two sisters competed constantly to hold the new baby. Lauren, seven at the time, became quite maternal. Leslie, four, viewed the new family member as a new doll.

At Lauren's birth, I started the tradition of writing yearly birthday letters to each of our children. But with each new child and the mounting responsibilities, I had less quiet time to write. It was November before I found time to sit down and reflect on Kelly's birth:

A TABLE FOR TWO

3 November 1985
Dear Kelly,

A few minutes alone is, to me these days, like precious water to a thirsty traveler. . .but I spend a little time each evening laying my hand on you and praying for God to bless you, protect and strengthen you, and fill you with discernment, love, and knowledge of himself. We picked the name, Kelly Marie, because we liked the sound of it, not because it means "warrior maid." But perhaps it will have special significance in the spiritual realm for you. Jesus said we are fighting against principalities, rulers of darkness. . . . Oh, Kelly, mothers always hold their children so close. I want to shield you, protect you from all this world holds to tempt and destroy you with. I release you to Jesus constantly. You're his, I know. I believe children born into Christian families are special agents of love in this dying age. Oh, my sweet, adorable little gal, may you grow to love him as he loves you! And to love what he loves, and hate what he hates.

We had all along been debating whether we'd like to have a third child. To me, a family of four just didn't feel "finished" or something. I can't explain it. So, finally, we prayed and decided to give God complete liberty to help us decide—and you might as well know it, a weekend without birth control—and I conceived the very first night! No question, little lady! He wanted you with us. . . .

My pregnancy with you went well for the most part. Six weeks into it, however, I got quite ill, with a fever of over 103. I had to do the music for a wedding, and, although Grandma couldn't believe I would do it, I didn't cancel out of it. (I was the only musician—soloist, accompanist, guitarist—everything! How would a bride feel if, on the day of her wedding, there was no music?) I did feel faint, however, but I made it through.

Lauren and Leslie and I spent the latter part of the pregnancy at the pool. With all that extra weight, it felt so good to float in the water! When, on the eve of July 29th, Braxton

Hicks contractions started, I felt pretty certain things were cooking. We went to bed early, telling your sisters that we might be gone in the morning, and that Grandma would be with them.

We called Grandma around 3:30 a.m., and reached the hospital by about 4:00. You were born almost six hours later, posterior position (turned a bit), but in fine shape. I had warded off hundreds of comments all summer: "Is this your boy? Are you trying for a boy?" It was hard to keep a neutral mind about it all, but when they said you were a girl, we could put it to rest. We were thrilled. Your doting sisters came and went each day, and the phrase, "Can I hold her?" continued to play like a broken record in this household.

Your temperament was a bit feistier than I'd been used to; at first we thought it might be a little colic—you'd have these five- to six-hour fussy periods, keeping us up until midnight and wearing our threads thin. But once in bed, you'd awaken only to eat. Not once to this day have you kept me up at night longer than to eat, and that's a joy! Now you're sleeping through the night, helped by the fall time change, so things are much more relaxed around here.

You love to talk to Daddy when he comes home, scrunching up your body and trying with all your might to make sounds back at him. We all watch you, captivated. And then the broken record begins from your sisters: "Can I hold her?" Sometimes it's hard to get a hold in edgewise!

Although you don't care a lot for the swing or for cuddling your face to my shoulder (you like to face out to see the action!), you are a delight, and are growing into such an alert, gregarious little person. We love you so much.

28 December 1986
. . .You've been asleep for three hours and haven't even changed positions. Each time I go in to check you, I can't resist stroking your head, your hair moist with the perspiration of warm, deep sleep.

This past year you've started to walk and to display a real sense of humor. I wish you could see your sisters rush to attend to your every need. I marvel at the closeness the three of you seem to share. Sibling rivalry is probably eventually a given, but how I hope this lasts. A couple of months ago, Lauren and Leslie were watching you outside a building into which I'd gone for a couple of minutes. When I came out, Lauren said you'd eaten a red berry off the bushes. Concerned, I called poison control, who recommended I give you Syrup of Ipecac. None of us knew it would make you sick for two days! Lauren could hardly forgive me for doing this to you . . . .

11 March 1988
. . . My intentions to write to my three lovely daughters once a year have been good, if not fully realized. Two-and-a-half! Where did our little baby go? Last year we moved to a new house, and you have adjusted well. Already you are a whiz at the card game, "Uno," can identify colors and numbers, and you love books. My, how you love books!

Last month you agreed to cooperate with potty training, and you're doing so well with it. One evening, as you were sitting quietly on my lap, watching with me a National Geographic special on gorillas, you looked up with the sweetest, most sincere little face and asked, "Do monkeys tinkle?"

"Uh-huh," I answered.

A few minutes went by, and you looked up again. "Do they poopie, too?"

"Yes, they poopie, too," I said, burying my nose in your soft, blonde hair and kissing you. Such are the tenderest moments a mother knows. I love to answer your questions, stare eyeball to eyeball with you, and meet the inquisitiveness of your soul. I love when you take my cheeks into your hands and turn my face toward you to force me to respond to those intensely wondering eyes. I love that you can verbalize your fears, your feelings, your gratitude, your wonder. . . .

Your personality is woven with strength. You are definitely able to fend for yourself, and it's that aspect of you which makes the times when you come for comfort or safety to Daddy or me all the more precious.

31 January 1992
    . . . I've become so negligent with these letters! But something happened two nights ago that I don't want to forget, or you to forget either. We were riding in the Toyota, on our way to pick up the station wagon from the garage in Manheim. (Remember, it got towed, and we were all so fascinated to watch?) Well, Daddy drove the fixed car home, and you and I headed for the mall to do a little shopping. As we waved good-bye to Daddy in the other car, you suddenly said, "On the way up here, I asked Jesus to come into my heart."

I looked at you, stunned. Daddy's and my conversation on the trip to the garage was totally unrelated—about finances or something. How is it that in the middle of that, you gave yourself a private altar call? "What made you think of doing that?" I asked.

You didn't respond. I looked over at you in the darkness, catching bits of light flickering off your face as we motored along down the highway. And then we got to talking about sin, the Holy Spirit, and the spiritual realm of the unseen hosts. Such questions you have! You wanted to know about angels. We discussed demons and calling on the name of Jesus when we're afraid. We talked of disobedience to God, even when we're Christians. You laughed when I said I struggle with disobedience in overeating. "It seems silly to think of eating as sin," you said. Some day, you'll understand these subtleties.

But for now, the joy of our intimacy, the preciousness of God's presence, and the unexpected blessing of this night are reasons for great thanksgiving.

This has been a neat year for you in first grade—taking off like wildfire with reading books. You read with incredible expression. Mrs. Neff has been such an encouragement to you in this. I don't know when I last read a book to you, but night-

ly (and whenever else you can corner a captive audience) you read to us.

This hasn't been an easy year for us. Resigning my music position after our church suffered a painful split has left us churchless for six months now—confused and bewildered. We're trusting God to tell us where he wants us, but sometimes it gets discouraging, and I wonder how it's all affecting you three girls. But tonight, what a testimony of God's work in your life in spite of this spiritual fog we're in. You can't imagine what a relief it is to know that Daddy and I are not alone in this parenting process. While he and I are fretting about finances, you're sitting in the back seat with Father/Mother God, drinking from the wells of salvation . . .

5.

The ambulance rumbled along the highway, picking up speed. "We've got to push it a little," the driver said. "We're late for your appointment."

I leaned wearily against the side wall, checking Kelly constantly with my eyes. She lay quietly, eyes closed, her head protruding from the end of her swaddled, strapped, mummy-like form. Teddy's worn pink head nestled in the crook of her neck. Behind us, though I could not see them, Rob, the girls, and his parents followed in a two-car caravan. With our increased speed, I assumed we lost them.

Philadelphia. The city hung in my memory like shades of gray. If I had been an artist, I would have mixed pigments of black and white all over my palette to portray my work: How Philadelphia Looks Through the Eyes of a Depressed Mother. I remembered a summer trip to the zoo when I was a child. Fumes, concrete, elephants, pigeons, and overcast skies. Gray, gray, gray. Today was no different. We pulled into the emergency entrance of Children's Hospital. Emerging from the ambulance, I looked up at the gray sky, down onto the gray concrete, and smelled fumes.

I stayed beside Kelly's head as the attendants asked where they should take her, and then walked alongside as they maneuvered the gurney into the lobby of the hospital. I immediately felt the big-city hospital commotion and a gruffer manner among the staff than at our local hospital. I was startled to see a McDonald's restaurant in the lobby. I noticed black people everywhere. Clearly, I came from too white a community if I observed that.

Kelly was wheeled to the far side of a room on the seventh floor, past a bed with a young girl lying quietly in it. "Hi, this is Nikeah," her young mother said softly to me. "She's six. She was hit by a car several days ago." Not feeling much like conversing, I briefly introduced Kelly, then prepared to settle into our side of the room.

I was relieved to discover I could stay with Kelly, sleeping on a sofa bed built into the wall under the windows. But after one look around, my heart sank. The TV on Kelly's side of the room, suspended from the ceiling, was shrouded in dust. Drink marks covered the phone table and dusty windowsill. I fought to keep my pooling eyes from spilling over.

I grabbed some wet paper towels and packaged alcohol pads from the sink in the bathroom and began to wipe everything. It was Saturday; housekeeping probably didn't work on the weekends, I told myself. They had accepted us as an emergency case on a floor already overcrowded. As I discovered later, this was not the housekeeping standard for the hospital. But at that point, with my lack of sleep, my stress, concern for Kelly, and my suspicion that we might have erred by coming here, this neglected room was not the environment I had hoped for.

Soon a resident from neurosurgery stopped by and put Kelly through a series of tests. I ached for her every time she had to get out of bed. When the doctor left, Kelly lay quietly. I talked to her reassuringly, no small feat in light of all my inner turmoil. I wanted to leave—flee back to the familiarity of our local hospital and friends.

Like a homesick camper seeing her family at week's end, I almost cried when Rob and Lauren appeared in the doorway a half hour later. They greeted Kelly cheerfully, then reported that Leslie, two years below the minimum age requirement for visiting, could not come up to the room. Kelly and I were heartsick. We pleaded gently with the nurse. "These sisters are Kelly's best friends and greatest supporters. We've come all the way from Lancaster. Please—is there any way she could be permitted to come up?"

Our nurse considered our request. "Has she had the chicken pox?" I nodded. "I'll see what I can do."

Meanwhile, Lauren and Rob went down to the lobby to be with Les while Rob's parents came up to be with Kelly. I left her in their care, grateful to be away from her so I could release my congested emotions. But in the crowded elevator and busy hallways, I still couldn't let it out.

My family was waiting for me at a table in front of McDonald's in the lobby. I unwrapped the breakfast sandwich they'd bought me and picked at it. Studying my face, Leslie lifted a napkin to my eyes. She had seen the trickles, and now her simple gesture of concern released the flood. But she didn't let me drown in it. "Mom," she said excitedly. "You have to come see the chapel we've found."

"In a minute," I said, gathering myself together, forcing another bite. I began to take in the lobby—seven stories of spaciousness. Suddenly I saw angels in all the corners and along the surrounding walls, joyously singing a hymn which mysteriously moved against my pain and called my heart to remember:

In thee is gladness amid all sadness, Jesus, sunshine of my heart.
By thee are given the gifts of heaven, thou the true Redeemer art.
Our souls thou wakest, our bonds thou breakest,
Who trusts thee surely hath built securely,
Naught can us sever, Hallelujah!

If He is ours, we fear no powers, nor of earth, nor sin, nor death.
He sees and blesses in worst distresses,
He can change them with a breath . . . .

A TABLE FOR TWO

I was unprepared for God's breath. Lauren and Leslie led me behind the elevators, past a circular wall, and then stood to either side of a set of glass doors. The look on their faces said, "You first, Mom," and so I entered. They quickly flanked me.

The doors gently closed behind us, shutting out the stir of the lobby. Enveloped in a carpeted, sacred silence, I felt their eyes eagerly search my face. I stopped in my tracks and drank in their gift. In front of us, in smooth white stone, was a statue of a kneeling mother, tenderly cradling the neck of a child about Kelly's size.

I hadn't expected God to write the answer to my soul's deepest question on the wall. But there it was, as though God had known I was coming and anointed an artist to prepare this for me. "Is all well with the child?" I read inscribed on the wall. My heart melted with the healing answer below it: "Yes, all is well."

My arms went out like the wings of a mother hen, and my daughters quickly settled under them. We moved together into the worship and meditation area. Pausing over an open notebook on a lectern, I read through my tears the words of heartsick parents who had been there before us. Humbly, I stood where they had been before, a newcomer preparing to walk the same cold, barren landscape:

"Dear God, please help Bobby keep his tubes in. This is so scary for him, and he's so little . . . "

"Father, Tasha needs Your healing touch. Be with her, and please comfort Ed . . ."

"God, I am so scared. I cannot bear this without You. Please get Randy a liver, and soon . . ."

We sat down and soaked in the stillness, the prayers of hundreds and hundreds of parents echoing off the walls, nearly audible in this oval room.

6.

Ma-Ma and Pop-Pop had managed to break through the intensity and infuse a little lightness into Kelly's room. Kelly sat propped up in her bed, enjoying a book being read to her when I walked back into the room.

"Three bites of a pancake and a couple sips of juice," Pop-Pop announced with thumbs up as he pointed to Kelly's breakfast tray. It was major intake for her. Soon Rob came in with Lauren—and Leslie.

"How'd you get Les up here?" I asked, elated.

"They gave us permission. The security guard was a little tough to get by, but finally he called up here and confirmed it with the nurses." Kelly smiled to see both sisters, and the three of them immediately took to the few toys and coloring books we had brought with us. In no time at all, Lauren and Leslie had succeeded in their self-appointed mission of drawing giggles from their weary comrade.

Moments later, a slender man with dark hair and a mustache stepped through the doorway. He greeted Kelly, then extended a hand to each of us. "I'm Dr. Sutton, neurosurgeon," he said. "Sorry I'm late. Saturdays I like to play golf." Rob's parents left the room as he sat down. "Yeah," he said, fumbling with his clipboard, "they keep telling me I best stay with my day job."

We relaxed under his casual manner. "So Kelly, how ya feel-in'?" he asked, smiling at her and putting his head back to allow her to study him. He conversed with her briefly; I gave thanks for his keen communication skills, so necessary in pediatrics.

Soon he was drawing diagrams of the brain, explaining tumor types most often found in this area in children of this age, and detailing the neurological risks of touching the brain stem in surgery. In spite of the comfortable, casual manner in which he reviewed it, the information was technical, frightening to me. He talked of problems that could result from nicking the brain stem even slightly: breathing problems that would necessitate a tracheotomy, impaired eye movement that might require subsequent surgery, and problems with balance and walking. "I won't know 'til I get in there whether the tumor has attached itself to the brain stem," he said. "It appears that it might have. When we go in, however, we take all our troops. Our goal is to aggressively get every last centimeter of tumor."

He flashed a playful look at Kelly. "She's tuning me out," he said, watching her crayoning her coloring book. "Kelly, I know what you're thinking. You have two questions. First, you want to know if you'll wake up in surgery, right?" She looked up, nodded, and eyed him cautiously. "And you want to know what kind of haircut I'm gonna give you." She smiled. He'd nailed her.

"The answer is that you absolutely will not wake up, and—" he motioned Lauren over and pulled her ponytail up on top of her head—"this is how much I'm gonna shave off." He made a horizontal line halfway between her neck and the top of her head. "See, then you can let the rest of your hair fall back down over it and hardly anyone will notice."

Kelly was satisfied and returned to her coloring. "One type of tumor," he continued, "is benign. We go in there and get it, and that's the end of your ordeal. I don't think it's that type, however. Another, medulloblastoma, is responsive to chemotherapy. If it's attached to the brain stem, and I have to leave some tumor behind, the chemo will probably take care of it. There've been great strides with this tumor type in the last five years. An ependymoma, however, while responsive to radiation, is affected least by chemotherapy, and so it's critical that we get all the tumor out, if possible."

The information weighed heavily on me. I was surprised he explained all of this in front of Kelly. He discussed it so matter-of-factly. *This is not just another brain,* I thought. *This is my daughter's head.* We were as comfortable with his consultation as two agonized parents could be under the circumstances. But when it came time to sign the consent form, I couldn't bear putting my signature to this invasive treatment. Rob signed. I was scared, crumbling inside.

"We'll operate, then, on Tuesday morning, three days from now," Dr. Sutton said, shaking our hands again.

Rob's parents, waiting for us, walked down the hall with us while we explained what the doctor had said. My chin quivered helplessly. "This is just so scary. I can't seem to stop crying."

My mother-in-law rubbed my shoulder gently. "Why don't you two go across the street to the hotel. We rented a room for you there. Just take a couple hours alone."

We didn't need much convincing. We went back to our kids, trying to smile brightly. "Daddy and I are going over to the hotel to check in and rest a bit. We'll be back a little later, okay?"

We felt each somber footstep we took down the hall. Rounding the corner out of the surgical wing to the hall adjoining the oncology floor, we saw two young girls about Kelly's age, leashed to IV poles. Bald, pale, and emaciated, they looked drained of life and vitality. We forced weak smiles as we passed. I thought of Kelly's beautiful, thick, smooth, blonde hair. No, God, no. *Not cancer. Not chemotherapy . . .*

I leaned for support against the corner of the inside of the elevator. The door slapped shut, confining us with a middle-aged woman. "You don't look so good," she said as she punched the button for the lobby and the elevator began its descent. "What's the matter?"

Weakly, I obliged her intrusion. "Our daughter has a brain tumor."

"Oh," she said flippantly, raising her arms and flinging her hands forward to brush it off. "Just give it to the Lord." The elevator came to a halt, and without so much as a backward glance at us, she thrust herself through the open door and dissolved into the crowd in the lobby.

Across the street from the hospital, we unlocked the door of our hotel room. Once it closed behind us, we were free—free to release the stormy prisoner—our emotions. Gone were the constraints of holding up for Kelly's sake, of being in-control parents for our other two daughters, of being dignified, functioning human beings in public. We slumped onto separate beds, unearthed the pillows, and let our hearts spill into them. We were wordless heaps, completely spent, crying for mercy.

When the high tide of emotion began to ebb, I lifted my head to consider my husband. In 18 years of marriage, I had seen him shed a few tears before, but I had never heard him weep. For a brief moment, I regarded him curiously.

Slowly, painfully, we began to form words over our wounds. "When Jesus was in the garden of Gethsemane, asking for the cup to pass," I said, "God, in all his love for his son, had to say no." The thought triggered a stinging surge of tears. Suddenly I understood the desperation of Christ's request, and God's horrific pain in having to deny it. We were Jesus, pleading for a way out. We were also the parent who could not provide a detour around the path that lay ahead.

The hotel beds became Mount Moriah, and we talked of Abraham surrendering Isaac on it. We reminded each other that all our children belonged to the Lord and recounted the day of Kelly's baby dedication. Back then we had made vows with arms tight around her. Now we were living those vows with arms that couldn't hold onto her.

"It hurts so much to think that I can't shield her from all this, can't protect her or help her," Rob said, succumbing to a fresh spasm of tears.

We faced our mutual horrors—surgery that may not end the ordeal but cause neurological impairment, and a pronouncement of cancer which would strip Kelly of her appearance and stamina, lengthen our time in Philadelphia, and wreak havoc on our family beyond what we could fathom being able to endure. The two bald girls in the hallway had sent a chilling signal to our brains. What about the risks of impaired eye movement, inability to walk, and a tracheotomy? *God, NO!*

"I could release her to death easier than I can release her to all that debilitating treatment," I choked. I wanted an escape. I didn't know what I was saying. Nor did I realize that we'd likely have to face both.

Our private pain partially diffused, I moved to Rob's bed where we joined hands in prayer. It was a Maundy Thursday prayer, and we were with Jesus in the garden of Gethsemane, feeling as much of his agony as we were humanly capable. Our lips moved as his had, "Father, if it be possible, let this cup pass . . ."

The plea went up like incense, absorbed into the silent expanse beyond. God's troublesome quiet! *Will you heal her? Will you take her?* The door to our Father's house seemed coolly closed. *God, no! Don't leave us!*

In that moment of feeling abandoned I began to comprehend, if only in a glimmer, that to lose our relationship with God would be worse than anything—absolutely *anything*—we'd be asked to part with or endure in this life. It must have been at the heart of Christ's response, too, for his prayer continued—as did ours—"Nevertheless, not our will, Lord, but yours be done."

Gradually over the next couple of hours, the storm passed. The wind within us, swirling and raging moments before, stilled. The clouds in our hearts, completely rained out, gave way to a hint of sunshine. We were ready to go back to our family.

A TABLE FOR TWO

Returning to Kelly, I felt fresher, able to look at her with encouragement instead of self-consumed agony. Then, while Ma-Ma and Pop-Pop stayed with her, Rob and I left with Lauren and Leslie for an early supper. Our ulterior motive was to talk with them alone. They had heard everything Dr. Sutton said. We guessed, correctly, that they were filled with questions and concerns, too.

We told them our fears and how intensely frightening this was for us. They admitted that they, too, were scared for Kelly—in fact, for themselves and the whole family. "It's like we're being asked to run a marathon," Lauren said, "when we haven't even trained for it."

Rob spent the night with Kelly, and the rest of us went to the hotel. I cried softly into my pillow, not wanting to concern Lauren and Leslie. I longed for a parent to tuck me in, pull the covers up to my chin, kiss my forehead, and tell me not to worry. I saw myself at a young age, remembering my parents entering the darkness and shifting the mattress slightly as they sat down beside me. "Anything you want to talk about tonight?" they would ask, the soft rustle of sheets and a squeak or two from the box spring filling in after the question as they adjusted the covers around me. I always had something. Sometimes a spider in a far corner of the room had me plastered to my bed in fear. Other times I feared the Soviet Union might bomb us during the night.

Mysteriously, I was always comforted. The spider either got squashed in a Kleenex or I had enough reason to trust that, at least for the night, no bombs would fall. And then the mattress popped up to level as they got up. I stretched my leg into the warm spot they left and listened for their footsteps moving down the hall, then going down the steps. It was a comforting decrescendo of sound, a benediction of sorts.

Tonight, my bed felt cold. There was no relief in knowing that both sets of our parents were as concerned and helpless as we were. "I know all the scriptures about waiting on you to renew strength, coming to you when heavy laden," I mouthed silently. "But I don't *feel* them. If you don't make these truths a reality in our emotions, none of us will get through this."

The scriptures, like cozy smoke rising from a country farm-house in winter, called me in from the cold. But when I knocked on the door, no one seemed to be at home. I tried the handle, slipped in, and hung my prayer like a hat on a hook in the kitchen.

7.

Philadelphia burst into color the next morning, the first day of summer. The sky a dazzling blue, the city splashed with sunlight, I filled my lungs with clean air as I crossed the street to the hospital.

Kelly was in good spirits. Her room felt more familiar, homey. When we left her in the care of her grandparents to get Rob out for a Father's Day walk around the nearby University of Pennsylvania, we were surprised to find ourselves laughing together. Whether they did it consciously or not, our daughters with their senses of humor and fun had pushed the gloom away. They invited our spirits to take a soaring balloon ride over our pain.

Off came my own shackles of gray. God, it seemed, had found what I hung on the hook in his kitchen and prepared a feast for our spirits, a drink in the desert, manna in the wilderness. We ate and drank gratefully, savoring the moment rather than worrying that there might not be enough food for the journey.

Returning to the hospital, we were happy to see our friends Jeff and Donna, who brought the healing warmth of friendship and an abundant basket of food. To Kelly the bookworm they presented a thick book of Calvin & Hobbes cartoons. As sick as she was, this gift, and many others she received, served manna to her in her private wilderness.

My brother and his family drove in for a visit from New Jersey. Later in the evening we said good-bye to them, and to Lauren and Leslie who went home with Ma-Ma and Pop-Pop. It had been a good day. The warmth of home had come to this environment, and we were greatly uplifted.

"This turned out to be a lot better Father's Day than I antici-pated," Rob said, flipping through the Calvin & Hobbes book to enjoy some cartoons with Kelly. Dragging a chair to the side of her bed, he opened the book, and they quickly cast themselves in the appropriate roles—Kelly as Calvin and Rob as Hobbes:

"It's July already! Oh no! Oh no!" Kelly read for Calvin, eyes wide and frantic. "What happened to June?! Summer vacation is slipping through our fingers like grains of sand! It's going too fast! We've got to hoard our freedom and have some more fun! Time rushes on! Help! Help!"

"I don't think I want to be here at the end of August," said the deep-voiced Hobbes.

"Aaugh! It's a half-hour later than it was half an hour ago," said Calvin frantically. "Run! Run!"

It was prophetic comedy. We had no idea then that the entire summer would slip through our fingers, almost entirely in Philadelphia. For the moment, however, we were gathering fuel for the hearth of our family, relishing the closeness, hold-ing the reins on our fear. *This sounds trite,* I recalled a friend who had a daughter suffering from leukemia saying, *but you have to live one day at a time. It's a mental discipline.*

When she wearied of reading, Kelly sank back into her pil-low. Eyeing her tenderly, we pulled up the covers, tucked teddy close beside her, and kissed them both on the nose.

She read our faces, and now the child comforted the parents. "Don't worry," she said soothingly. "I'm not afraid of surgery."

By the next afternoon, however, on the day before surgery, we were anxious, irritable. Kelly had yet another MRI—this one for research purposes—followed by the pronouncement that the day after surgery she would have still another, to determine whether all the tumor had been removed. If not, they would reenter the brain while the opening was still fresh. The thought made me shiver, along with the possibility that she might be neurologically impaired. We were riding a fast moving wave of surrender. There was no turning around. Without the surgery, she would certainly die.

Pastor Tom and his wife Dori arrived for a morning visit. Later, my parents came. While we appreciated their presence, we were edgy, preoccupied. Helpless and worried themselves, they could do little but love us from the sidelines, watch, and pray.

Rob left early that evening so Kelly and I could get a good night's rest before her operation. "I love you, Trooper," he said, kissing her good-night. "I'll see you bright and early tomorrow morning."

Tucked in by 10:00 p.m., I studied Kelly's face in the semi-darkness. I watched her put her hands on her temples and press gently. I remembered her telling me that it helped her dizziness when her eyes were shut. Soon, her right hand dropped to her side, and her left hand fingers began to stir rhythmically in the hole in teddy's left ear. The hole and his worn fur told the story of six years of soothing comfort. I thought back to the night before her birth. Now I wondered if God's hand had been more prophetically involved in our naming her than I had thought.

My mind drifted to the family room of our home two years before. Kelly had turned on a tape of worship music and begun a dance to it—a graceful interpretation of the music, free and artistic, totally unself-conscious in my presence as I read the newspaper. Suddenly, with no cue from the music, she went to the opposite corner of the room and began to beat the air with her fists. After a few moments, she returned to the original corner and resumed her graceful dancing. She continued to alternate between the two dances for some time.

I watched out of the corner of my eye, inconspicuously, so

as not to disturb this four-year-old's unusual display of expression. But I was too curious to keep quiet. "Kelly, your graceful dance over in that corner is so beautiful," I had said. "But I don't understand what you're doing in the other corner. It doesn't seem to fit the music."

"Over here," she said, twirling to the corner with expressive grace and continuing her movement, "I'm dancing to God because He loves me." She then leaped to the other corner and beat her fists into the air. "Over here, I'm fighting the devil because he's trying to kill me."

It was the kind of comment that a mother assimilates with a tremor of astonishment, suddenly realizing that her young child, from whom she has been largely inseparable, is an independent being with independent thoughts and an individual spirituality. While we had showered our family life with talk of God's love, we had purposely avoided any burdensome conversation about evil in our children's presence, even as it became an issue for us through books or occult activities practiced by students at the high school where Rob was a counselor. I had the distinct awareness at that moment that she had been given spiritual knowledge beyond what she had been taught by us or others in her life.

Warrior maid, I thought on this critical night before surgery. *What a strange, weakened way to begin battle.* I wondered what God was doing here. The vision, the dance—was God preparing me? Was the devil really trying to kill her?

The questions were deep and terrifying. I plunged my thoughts into Psalm 131 and mentally recited the soothing words to anchor my troubled spirit: *I do not concern myself with great matters, or things too wonderful for me, but I have stilled and quieted my soul; like a weaned child with its mother, like a weaned child is my soul within me . . .*

I awoke at 11:40 in disbelief. "You're going to do *what?*" I asked groggily. I reached for my glasses and brought into focus a large, burly man wearing hospital scrubs.

"I'm very sorry to have to disturb your sleep," he said, "but we need another blood sample before Kelly's surgery. Unfortunately, not enough was taken for testing this afternoon."

With arms as big as flour canisters, he scooped Kelly up and gently carried her across the hall into the treatment room. "Kelly," he whispered tenderly, setting her down on a table, "I hear you're the nicest girl on the floor up here. Is that true?"

He smiled kindly and drew the blood gently and efficiently. His manner was so soothing that he elicited not the slightest whimper of protest from her. Tucked back in bed, she easily fell back to sleep.

8.

"Are you ready, Trooper?" Rob entered the room with his thumb up in the air, then bent to kiss Kelly's forehead.

Kelly smiled peacefully. We prepped her about how the events of the morning would unfold and promised her we'd be there the minute she came out. "You're going to have a wonderful sleep during surgery," I said. "When you wake up in ICU, though, your head will probably hurt. The nurses there know just what to do to help the pain."

"Why don't we pray together," Rob suggested, reaching for Kelly's Bible. Purposely opening to Psalm 91, Kelly's favorite passage, he began to read: "If you make the Most High your dwelling—even the Lord, who is my refuge—then no harm will befall you, no disaster will come near your tent . . ."

No disaster will come near your tent. The verse triggered a scene in my memory—October 1991—six months before the onset of Kelly's illness. Rob was gone for the evening, and the kids and I had just finished eating supper. "Girls, come over here into the family room and sit down for a few minutes," I said. "The dishes can wait. I want to read you something."

We didn't often read together as an entire family, but a particular story from *Guideposts* magazine struck me, and I thought its poignant application of scripture would make an interesting devotional reading for all of us.

A husband and wife were camping in the Adirondacks of New York. During the night, a baby bear wandered into their campsite, looking for food. Scared off by a loud sound caused by his own mischief, he fled the area. Moments later, his enormous and angry mother appeared. She began tearing up the campsite, growling intensely, ripping apart the campers' backpacks.

Obeying the instructions of the park ranger, the couple clanged pots and pans together to scare her away. But one of the metal bowls had leftover chocolate pudding in it, and, instead of fleeing, the bear charged the tent, pressing her weight against it.

The terrified woman was close enough to smell the growling bear's breath. She found herself saying some words from the Psalms out loud in the middle of this assault: "No evil shall befall you. No evil shall befall you." Then an amazing thing happened. A breeze began to blow upwind of their tent and scent, and the bewildered bear barged off into the brush.

The author looked up the verse—in her bear-clawed Bible— that had come so mysteriously to her. She knew it was part of Psalm 91, but what amazed her was the second half of the verse: "No evil shall befall you, *and no disaster come near your tent.*"

When I finished reading the story, Kelly went over to the bookshelf and got her new Bible. "Help me find that verse, Mommy," she said. While I opened to it, she got several highlighters, then proceeded to cover the entire text in rainbow colors.

Weeks later she had memorized the passage and often quoted it at nighttime before praying with one of us. It was a story that brought scripture to life in a young child's heart, and she would never forget its application. From that night on, and especially as she grew in her ability to read, Kelly became a lover of the scriptures. Rainbow colors began to appear in all parts of her Bible.

Now, as Kelly lay vulnerable at the door of her tent, Rob continued the passage: "For he will command his angels concerning you to guard you in all your ways—" I could see Rob struggling to keep his composure. Finally, we joined hands and prayed.

"'Gimme a peace,' Lord, is what Kelly used to pray before bed when she was little," I prayed. "And now, we ask for the same. Give her peace. Let her sense your nearness even as she is asleep in surgery. We entrust her to you, we put this surgery into your hands, and we make you, the Most High, her dwelling and ours. Although we don't understand why all this has to happen, we know that you love each of us deeply, and that somehow you'll use all of this for your glory."

We had just finished praying when we heard the clatter of attendants coming with the gurney to the doorway. Rob offered to carry Kelly out to the hallway. Slowly, with reverent tenderness, he lifted her from her bed and, cradling her to his heart, made the few steps to the awaiting transport. It was a helpless father's last protective gesture. As he was later to tell me, he felt like Abraham laying Isaac on the altar at the top of Mount Moriah.

We accompanied her down to the surgical floor, where we were instructed to remain in a designated waiting area until they came for her. "Daddy," Kelly said, "will you do me a favor?"

We were her servants, poised to walk to the ends of the earth for her. We leaned closer to make sure we picked up every last bit of her request.

"Don't call me 'Trooper' anymore, okay?" She rolled her eyes disgustedly, then grinned. We laughed, grateful for a little comma of relief in all the intensity.

Soon a friendly attendant came to take her and teddy to the operating room. We waved good-bye and did a thumbs up. Then, as she disappeared through the double doors, we turned to catch a glint of tears in each other's eyes.

A TABLE FOR TWO

We prepared for a wait of up to five or six hours, first by moving our belongings out of Kelly's room and into storage. We would get a new room assignment following her recovery in ICU. Encouraged by the nurses to take our time and eat a good breakfast, we went back to the hotel. After eating, we met with my parents, sister, and two pastor friends up in our room for prayer.

We all held hands in a circle as sunlight streamed through the windows and words of faith and hope ascended from the lips of the group. My attention was riveted across the street on what was happening with Kelly, and I was anxious to return to the parents' waiting room. Restless, I opened my eyes and looked around at everybody. Then I saw a teardrop roll down the side of my father's nose, glistening in the sunlight before it fell to the floor. I was so caught up in my own agony, I had forgotten how deeply others were feeling it, too. In many ways Rob and I were also like the "sick" mentioned in the anointing service, and the prayers of these faithful people were saving us, too.

Finally back at the hospital, we looked for the woman who had identified herself as the informational liaison between the operating room and the waiting room. Her job was to keep us updated and informed. She soon found us. "They're a little behind schedule," she said smiling, "but they've got her head shaved and are soon ready to go."

Our prayer group whiled away the minutes by reading, visiting, and playing quiet games. I didn't feel much like talking, so I spent the time writing instead. After only two and a half hours, the waiting room attendant appeared in the doorway. We looked up immediately.

"Dr. Sutton's closing her up," she said. "He should be out in about 15 minutes."

Stunned by the brevity of the operation, we imagined the worst. What if they couldn't remove the tumor at all, or what if it was hopelessly attached to the brain stem?

"Do you know anything else?" I asked. "We were told it would take much longer than this."

"I'm sorry, but that's all I know. I'm only informed of the progress of the surgery. I never make reports of any other kind."

Our games and conversation pulled to an anxious halt. Silence fell over us, none of us knowing how to feel.

Our eyes seized Dr. Sutton's familiar face the moment he came through the doorway. Wearing scrubs he sat down before us. Gradually, he uncorked the pressure we'd built up in our minds, telling us that he felt fairly certain they had resected the entire tumor. We were elated to hear him say it had not attached to the brain stem except at two tiny places which he easily severed.

"There's still a question as to the composition of the tumor," he said. "It will be several days before we are certain and can make an accurate diagnosis. She'll definitely need further treatment, but I can't say exactly how much until the pathology report is back."

We celebrated, but with reservation. Then we discovered that Rob's parents had brought Lauren and Leslie back to the hospital. "We just couldn't stay away," the girls said, "not while all this was going on." Relieved and ever-encouraged to see them, I felt badly that I was so removed from their lives and concerns. I was barely able to manage my own responses to this ordeal, and I had little time or stamina to help them.

Two hours later we were permitted to see Kelly in ICU. Two at a time, we went to be with her. Her hair swept up on top of her head, she lay on her back, eyes closed, covered only with a sheet.

"Kelly," I said gently, touching her feet and stroking them lightly. "Mommy and Daddy are here." She groaned in response. "It's okay, honey. We're going to stay right here beside you. You just rest; the nurses are taking good care of you."

She was hooked up to all kinds of computerized monitors. I

watched the waveforms slide rhythmically across the screens. Lauren and Leslie came in, each one working hard to soothe her with their presence.

That evening, everyone encouraged me to get a good night's rest at the hotel, rather than to try to sleep in the rocking chair beside her bed. Kelly moaned in protest as I said good-night. "There are no beds in here for me, sweetie," I spoke softly, my heart torn. "The nurses will take good care of you, and, if they need me, they know where to reach me. I'll see you bright and early in the morning."

When the doctor examined her the next day, Kelly groaned irritably at his many requests for her to move. "Good sign," he said. "She's responding as she should." With that, he discharged her onto the surgical floor.

As we were awaiting transport, a boy just out of surgery was wheeled into the space beside Kelly's bed. Similar to Kelly in size, he lay on his side, revealing a bandage up the back of his shaven head. I personally knew no other child on earth who had a brain tumor, and I was curious to know if this young fellow was going through what we were.

There was barely time to even glance at his parents, a handsome black couple who came in just as we were leaving. I didn't know it then, but I had just passed the woman, his mother, who would become my closest Philadelphia friend.

Kelly was transferred to a private room at the end of the hall. I rejoiced in the refreshing freedom of not having the TV on constantly, as it had been in our previous room. Rob brought our things, and we settled in for what we knew would be at least a week of recuperation. By suppertime, Kelly asked for her teddy bear, and we were thrilled to provide this small comfort for her.

The next day was a quiet, restful one for both Kelly and us, except for the disturbance of having to go for another MRI to check for residual tumor. That evening Dr. Sutton came to our door. This time he called us into the hall to talk away from Kelly's hearing. As he spoke, I felt my body withering under key words: medulloblastoma, radiation, chemotherapy, 15-month treatment protocol. With barely a comma for breathing in between, we were having to move from adjusting to the need for brain surgery to the reality that our six-year-old daughter had cancer.

"There's no question about it," Dr. Sutton said, eyeing me. "This is very tough on families physically and financially." He paused briefly, then went on to laud the results of the operation. "The good news is she didn't get messed up in surgery. Her neurological functions aren't impaired. She's responding well, and the treatment, while it may seem long, is effective in many cases."

Kelly was sleeping when we went back into the room. I leaned against Rob and cried quietly, the warmth of his body comforting the feverishness I felt. He had expected this, he told me. I, however, hadn't allowed myself to think further than the surgery.

A nurse came into the room to check Kelly. Regarding me briefly, she came over to the chair into which I had slumped and knelt before me. Taking my hands in hers, she spoke softly, tenderly. "I know it seems impossibly hard right now, but in a year things will look so different." I released one hand to wipe the tears of gratitude at her simple act of mercy. "We see kids all the time who come back to visit, and they're doing great. The oncology kids and staff really get to know each other, and they're like one big family."

Her gentle words of encouragement were a momentary topical anesthetic. But once she had gone, our minds blazed with strategizing in spite of our pain. Lauren's words rang in my head: *a marathon . . . a marathon . . . We're being asked to run a marathon, and we haven't even trained . . . haven't even trained . . . trained . . .* I imagined the grueling miles and the stressed limbs. I saw our family tearing apart at the seams. Already I felt the strain of what these hospitalizations had done to us. But nothing gripped me as terrifyingly as picturing Kelly stripped of her appearance and stamina. I held her silky blonde hair in my mind, only to watch it slip like gold dust through my fingers.

It was late, time for Rob to return to his newly acquired room at the Ronald McDonald House. I could see in his face that he was holding up for my sake and would soon have his own moments alone in his bed. We held each other, two saplings struggling to stay rooted in a violent storm.

Kelly continued to sleep while I prepared for bed. I pondered the words of Jesus as he fielded the question about why one man was born blind: "Rabbi, who sinned, this man or his parents, that he was born blind?"

"Neither this man nor his parents sinned," Jesus replied, "but this happened so that the glory of God might be displayed in his life."

. . . *the glory of God. That's the reason for all this. For the glory of God.*

The words from this passage had rung in my spirit one week ago, and now they rang deeper and louder. *God, we have released this situation to your glory,* I prayed. *Not what we would choose, though you know our agonizing desire.*

My thoughts turned the pages of all the scripture I had laid up in my heart over the years, and I drank deeply of it, simultaneously soothed and troubled. Had my vision of Kelly lying dead in a bed been like Simeon telling Mary, at the circumcision of the infant Jesus, that *a sword will pierce your soul?*

I began to absorb, more penetratingly than ever, what I knew in my head but had not yet experienced with my heart: that none of my children belonged to me. Each had been given a purpose uniquely her own, and I could exert little or no control over that. Like Mary, I could only live fully by responding, *I am the Lord's servant. May it be to me as you have said.*

My thoughts turned again to the garden of Gethsemane. I looked into the face of God and realized that in his deepest, most perfect love, he may have to refuse my plea.

For the glory of God.

9.

Early the next morning we were told it was time to take off the bandage. Kelly whined and protested. The doctor assured me her irritability was normal and a good sign. It didn't make the process easier, however. Quickly, the nurses stripped off the bandage, revealing a six- to eight-inch incision with zipper-like stitches lining it from top to bottom. Looking at it sent a shiver up my spine.

Rob soon arrived looking weary. "A rough night," was all he said.

"We're scheduled to meet with the oncology team at 2:00 this afternoon," I told him.

Kelly had a hard morning with mood swings and irrational kicking and screaming. But by afternoon, she was markedly different. At the designated time of our meeting, we left her in the care of our friend Donna and followed a team member to the conference room. The discussion was technical, difficult to grasp.

"You mean she doesn't have a medulloblastoma?" I asked.

"The pathology lab did a more intricate test, indicating ependymomal properties to the tumor. Five years ago this kind of test wasn't done, and we would still have called it a medulloblastoma. But, yes, we are changing the diagnosis. Arriving at the correct diagnosis makes all the difference in the treatment plan we choose."

"So what does this mean?"

"Since ependymomas are not responsive to chemotherapy, we are recommending radiation only, for six weeks this summer."

"You mean no chemotherapy?"

"Correct."

I felt elated. Greatly relieved. But I was centered more on the inconvenience of the treatment plan than I was the severity of her illness. "I feel happier. Should I be happier?"

"Well, the treatment plan is definitely shorter." But nobody was smiling.

We inquired as to what her prognosis might be. Based on a survival rate of living five more years, the doctors indicated a 30-40% chance of surviving that long for most children with ependymomas. "But in many of those cases, the entire tumor was not able to be resected," the doctor told us. "In Kelly's case, the complete resection could double her chances."

When we returned to Kelly, we were feeling somewhat better, based on this lesser treatment sentence and a reasonably positive outlook. Kelly had a stellar afternoon and evening. She tried sitting up in a chair, and she read aloud from Calvin & Hobbes. And she took in her first food in four days: a few French fries with ketchup, three or four M&M's, a few bites of pizza, and half a plum.

After supper she talked on the phone with Lauren and Leslie. Our conversations with them always freshened our perspective, reminding us that life still had its normal aspects. They got Tucker near the phone and made him bark. Kelly missed him desperately. Finally we had to say good-bye to Rob, too, who went back to Lancaster to be with the girls and take care of things there.

That night Kelly kicked and cried and fought stubbornly with the bed pan. The sheets and my arm got soaked in the process. She screamed while the bed got changed. Morning brought more of the same. Finally around noon, she calmed down. With her eating and drinking improved, the nurses capped her IV and she was free. Our big assignment for the day was to walk.

Hair still high on her head, sticky with operating room goo, Kelly took a nurse's arm on one side and mine on the other. Teetering with every step, we inched our way down the hall. "Her balance will get better and better," the nurse assured me. "The cerebellum is your center of balance, and that's the area that got cut into the most in surgery. It will improve, though. You'll be surprised."

That afternoon my cousin Sally arrived from home, and, with her unique humor, she got Kelly giggling. It was so wonderful to have laughing in the room and to hear Kelly say in the bathroom, "Sally really brings the smiles out of me." Kelly not only joined in the conversation, she was Miss Motormouth. It was a healing afternoon. I tried desperately to savor it all.

But the next morning the pendulum swung in the opposite direction. After a bathroom visit, Kelly experienced severe dizziness and a headache, after which she vomited twice. She refused to eat. I started to fear hydrocephalus, fluid build-up in the brain. The medical community was forever quizzing her about headaches. I felt scared, teary again. I cried out for God's sheltering wings.

A friend from home called as if in response to my prayer. Comfort poured out of her words. God was near. The afternoon once again brought improvement, and when Rob brought Lauren and Leslie after supper, Kelly perked up dramatically. I could hardly believe she was the same person.

"Kelly," Lauren said with a smile on her face, "we've brought you a very special present." She looked at Leslie with a secretive grin as she pulled a tiny plastic bag out of a paper sack. "It's the closest we could bring Tucker to you."

Kelly took the plastic bag which was filled, we all now realized, with Tucker's soft, collie fur. "Oh . . ." she said tenderly, taking the clump out of the bag and holding it up to her cheek.

"Oh, sweetie . . . I miss you so much." She closed her eyes and kept the fur at her cheek, savoring his scent.

My brother Andy called, wanting to take me out to dinner with his wife and daughter. So while my family entertained Kelly, I went with them for a walk around the city to find a restaurant. It was my first lengthy trip outside the hospital walls in days, and I absorbed the outdoors, especially pleased when we found a sidewalk patio restaurant. It was refreshing to be out, to be cared for, and to watch the antics of my two-year-old niece, Sarah. I had been with sick children so long that I was losing my vision of healthy children.

The following day I wrote in my journal, "An UP! day!" Kelly awoke in fairly good spirits. While she watched TV in the morning, Willie came into the room to do his daily mop of the floor.

"Willie," I said, watching him meticulously get into the corners and clean up every stray piece of dirt, "you do such a wonderful job. You're the best housekeeper I've ever seen. You treat us like royalty."

He kept right on mopping, then melted my heart with his response. "I just tell myself to think what it would be like if it were my own child in that bed, and that keeps me going."

"You're an extraordinary man, Willie." He told me about his recovery from alcoholism while he finished. When he left, my heart felt noticeably refreshed.

Kelly made great progress that day, with the loving encouragement of physical and occupational therapists. My moods, I realized, had everything to do with how she was doing, and this day of improvement lightened my heart significantly. While still fairly shaky on her feet, Kelly was getting stronger. We slept fairly well that night.

The next morning I took a look at Kelly's sticky hairdo and asked the nurse if there was any way we could wash it. "Sure," she said. "I'll see if the bathtub is free."

It took an hour, and it took both of us to support her head so that we wouldn't get any water on the incision. But when she was finished, it was a great relief to all of us. Meticulously, I combed through the long wet strands, avoiding the incision area. A quick blow-dry, and Kelly looked fresher and much healthier.

That afternoon Dr. Goldwein, radiation oncologist, arrived. He chatted with Kelly briefly, then informed me of the continuing discussion among the oncology staff about how to treat Kelly's tumor type most effectively. Apparently the team felt that even though the tumor had ependymomal properties, they wanted to cover all bases and give Kelly the best chance possible.

"We're now recommending radiation *and* chemotherapy," he said apologetically. "I'm very sorry for all this confusion."

His words knocked the wind out of me. "Is this the final decision, or is it going to change again?"

"This is the final decision. Again, I know this has been hard for you. We're very sorry. But we want to give Kelly every opportunity to get well."

The emotional roller coaster dipped to a new low again. I fought tears while I was in Kelly's presence. Fortunately, her first-grade teacher, Mrs. Neff, had planned to come, and she entered the room at just the right time.

We visited with her, and then invited her husband and two young daughters to eat with us in the cafeteria. Tired of her hospital trays, Kelly was glad to substitute Pizza Hut pizza in the cafeteria, a meal for which she received a coupon to replace her hospital dinner.

That evening after the Neffs had gone, we watched the local news. Rumblings that a strike was forthcoming by CHOP's union hospital workers were growing louder. Would there be a strike by the midnight deadline? The nurses had talked to us about this. They told us it involved housekeeping, food service, some aides, and a few technicians, but that contingency plans were already in place, should the strike occur. With enough to worry about, I didn't focus on it too intently.

"What are you doing?" Kelly asked, observing me writing in a little notebook after we turned off the TV.

"I'm journaling."

"What's journaling?"

"It's when you tell what happened during the day, and how you feel about it."

"Can I journal, too?"

I looked up at her. "I think that would be a wonderful idea." I got her paper and pencil, and we wrote together for quite some time.

"I'd love to read what you wrote, Kelly. But journals can be private, so if you don't want me to read it, that's okay."

She handed me her paper. "I don't mind. I want you to read it."

30 June 1992

> "It is 9:45 at night, it is a very pleasant night at the hospital, except for the screaming in the next room. I feal very good, but a little worried, about the situation I am in right now." "I seem to be pretty ready for it, but do not know all the details yet." "And I also feal a little scared about the whole situation to." "It is hard for me to control my feelings but I feel a little better because I let my feelings out." but I also know that God is with me guiding and protecting me. and that makes me feel a whole lot better.

Touched deeply by her words, I climbed into her bed and snuggled close to her. It was the first time we had hugged in over a week. Both of us needed it. "This is cozy and feels nice, Mommy," she said, sighing contentedly.

We talked about our anxieties and our fears. Then, clasping hands, we prayed, resting gratefully under God's almighty wings. God fed us deeply, and Kelly drifted off to sleep.

I carefully moved out of her bed and went to my own, taking out the walkman that Cindy, the social worker, had lent me. I sank back into the pillow, set the earphones on my head, and turned on the music. When I heard the first strains, I realized I hadn't listened to any music in over a week. Like soft rain on dry ground, the lyrics softened my soul . . .

I've always heard there is a land beyond the mortal dreams of man
Where ev'ry tear will be left behind, but it must be in another time.
There'll be an everlasting light shining a purest holy white,
And ev'ry fear will be erased, but it must be in another place . . .

The events of the last two weeks played like a movie collage in my mind, as the sound track wove tender strands of God's love around the pain:

So I'm waiting for another time and another place,
Where all my hopes and dreams will be captured with one look at
    Jesus' face.
Oh, my heart's been burnin', my soul keeps yearnin',
Sometimes I can't hardly wait for that sweet, sweet someday . . .

I saw the faces of the medical personnel, passing before me with our family and friends like characters in the movie, and I saw God's mighty hand in all their caring, their skill, and their dedication. I drifted off to sleep like Kelly—a child at peace in the storm.

10.

I awoke with a start. Checking my watch, I saw it was 1:00 a.m. Loud rioting had roused me. In my mental fog, I struggled to assess what was happening. Then it hit me. The strike! I lay there for quite some time, marveling that I could hear all this so distinctly from seven floors up and in the rear of the hospital. Poor Willie. Pulled by virtue of his position and forces beyond himself into this fiery fray, he had to be torn apart inside.

I was annoyed that my peaceful night of sleep was now utterly disturbed. But then I thought of other parents in crisis situations like ours, here for their first night. If this had happened one week earlier, I can only imagine how I would have managed to transcend all the turmoil.

The hospital was buzzing with rumors the next morning. Some said picketers—with forces augmented by outside insurrectionists—blocked ambulances from coming into the emergency entrance and threw a brick through a supply room window. The nurses, on a delayed shift, carried on with calm professionalism. Kelly and I had looked forward to being discharged after a morning MRI, but the scan was rescheduled for late in the evening and our discharge postponed until the following day.

Profoundly disappointed, I called Rob immediately to stop him and the girls from coming for us. We had been primed for our grand return home; I wanted each and every day there to count before we had to return to Philadelphia for the summer. Now, with security so tight, it felt like we were locked in and the world locked out.

In an effort to make amends to patients and their families for the stress and inconvenience of the strike, the hospital treated us to supper served by the Marriott Hotel, the hospital's contingency food providers.

Around 9:30 p.m., transport came to pick up Kelly for the MRI. I sat with her like always, by now bored with the whole procedure, since this was our fifth one in two weeks. Kelly was bored, too, and very sleepy.

"This is going to take nearly two hours," our technician told us. "We'll be doing a complete scan of the head and spine."

Most children receiving an MRI were sedated, I had noticed. But since Kelly did so well, I requested no sedation for any of the scans. "What happens if she falls asleep in there?" I asked. "She's really tired."

Kelly did snooze for about an hour. But suddenly, in the middle of one of the lengthier pictures, she began to stretch, lifting her teddy with one arm and trying to turn. The technician mouthed to me an expletive of some sort and then threw her hands up in the air and laughed. She came in and powered Kelly out of the tube. Kelly was perspiring, so I fanned her while she groaned from having her good sleep disrupted.

"Do we have to do the whole thing over again?" I asked.

"No, just that picture, thankfully."

"Kelly," I said. "Wake up. You were sleeping, and then you stretched your arms and legs. You can't do that, or she'll have to keep taking the pictures over and over again. Can you please try to stay awake and lie real still?"

She did well the rest of the time, and we went back to our room, elated that after one more night of sleep, we would be released.

The morning brought Rob, the girls, and great anticipation. We packed our clothes, leftover snacks, and Kelly's gifts, and waited for our discharge orders to be written. Finally, after an hour, I inquired whether they had been written.

"Yes," the nurse told me. "All we need yet is a signature from the doctor."

We waited another hour while Rob packed the car. I asked again.

"Oh, you haven't gotten them yet? I'm sorry, I'm not sure what happened. I'll notify the resident." A half hour later she reported that the sought-after resident had gone to lunch. "You might as well get some lunch yourself. We'll try to have the papers signed by the time you get back."

When we returned, there was yet another delay. The stress I had built up over the weeks took its toll, and my anger rolled out in the form of tears. "I'm sorry," I said. "I'm just so tired of all this bureaucracy. We've not been home in two weeks, and all we want to do is go home. You've all been wonderful, but it shouldn't take four hours to try to get out of here." The nurse was extremely apologetic. And, miraculously, our discharge papers appeared—pronto.

The outdoors looked wonderful to me, even as we rolled along the Schuylkill Expressway with all its fumy, heavy traffic and gray concrete everywhere. But when we approached Lancaster County, I cried when I saw the rolling green farmland. Everything looked so new, so fresh. We pulled into our driveway, and my emotions overflowed as I read a huge sign, the length of our two garages: "Welcome Home, Kelly!"

Within a day, I began to grasp the tremendous caring concern going on around us. I couldn't stop weeping each time somebody brought us something. Our neighborhood gathered a sunshine box full of gifts for Kelly; the church collected another, this time with presents for the rest of the family, too. One woman cleaned our house while we were in Philadelphia.

I was enormously touched, because, with her creative gifts, she was the last person I expected to do this. She laughed when I thanked her. "Yeah, it is pretty ironic. Here I am cleaning your house while my cleaning lady cleans mine."

Home was wonderful. Family was heavenly. Tucker was joyous. Simple routines, void of hurtful medical procedures and disconcerting news, became joy-replenishing tasks. Hard as I tried, however, I couldn't mentally stretch the time at home to the length I needed it.

Kelly and I were not in good moods the morning my mother came to pick us up for the return day trip to Philadelphia. Dr. Sutton would remove the stitches; Dr. Janss, our neuro-oncologist, was going to give Kelly a spinal tap. Ependymomas, we were told, can seed themselves in the cranial/spinal fluid, so the spinal tap was to determine whether cancer cells were present in her spine. In spite of our internal compasses pulling in the opposite direction, off we went. There was no turning back.

Removing the stitches was painful for Kelly. Several of them were especially difficult to get out. When a nurse attempted to give Kelly some sedation for the spinal tap through a needle in her arm, Kelly turned hysterical with fear. She, too, had had it with all this.

Dr. Janss came into the treatment room, sympathetic and ever accommodating. "Oh Kelly," she said. "Enough of this. I feel so bad that you're so upset." She put her arm around her and kissed the top of her head. "How 'bout we try something else. It takes longer, but I have a pill you can take that will calm you down a little, okay?"

Kelly took the pill, but after a half hour she was still too upset to submit to the spinal tap. Lying on the table, she began to cry. I tried to calm her with talk about Tucker. Nothing worked. Finally I looked her in the eye. "Kelly, it's almost closing time for the nurses here. We have to get this over with, or we'll be here all night. Please? How 'bout we ask Jesus to help you?"

A TABLE FOR TWO

I prayed for her. Then Dr. Janss entered and said, "I have one more option. It's a bit of a disinhibiting drug that I think will do the trick. It might make her—" she smiled and cupped her hand over her mouth, whispering to me "—like a sloppy drunk."

It worked. Afterwards we headed for the car, totally spent. On the way home, I began to witness signs of the medicine's disinhibiting properties. While my mother drove, I stayed in the back seat where I hoped Kelly would sleep. Unable to be contained in a seat belt, she grew restless, climbing up on the shelf of the rear window, grinning and saying silly things. Then, after making a feeble attempt at falling asleep, she put her head in my lap and began to cry.

"Mommy," she said, her chin quivering, her voice desperate. "How can I show Lauren and Leslie how much I love them? I love them so much, I want to show them how much."

The sentiment was touching, even if the drug was largely responsible for it. But what came out of her immediately thereafter broached an area which caused me to forget about the drug entirely. "Mommy," she said, taking my face in her hands and turning it toward her pleading eyes. "Why would God let me get a brain tumor? Doesn't he love me?" She began to sob into my shoulder.

She had asked the question that hung like a weight in the pit of all our beings. Until now, no one dared acknowledge it or voice it out loud. Pierced to the depths, I couldn't answer her. I held her close and cried with her—into her hair—deep, wrenching tears. My mother, observing us in the rearview mirror, began to cry, too.

I don't know why, child . . . I don't know why!

11.

Our next respite at home was six days long, before we had to return to Philadelphia for radiation simulation. Kelly's walking improved daily, although I still helped her up and down steps. "Wanna walk to the store with me for some milk?" I asked her one pleasant afternoon. "I'll get you a Slushy, if you want."

Hand-in-hand, we walked down our quiet suburban street. "Your birthday's just a few weeks away," I said excitedly. "You'll be seven—wow!"

Kelly was quiet, thoughtful. "Mommy?'

"What, sweetie?"

"Could I . . . Could I die from this?"

It had finally come, the question I knew we had to talk about sooner or later—the question I had been bleeding over daily. I struggled to dam up the cascade of tears that threatened to spill over in response to it. "Some people die of cancer, but many do not," I began carefully, grateful to be walking beside her rather than being face-to-face when she would see my nose reddening and ask for the umpteenth time, "Mommy, are you crying?" I simply could not bear the concern my tears caused her.

I named two people I knew who had cancer and now led cancer-free lives. "The fact that they removed all your tumor and that you'll be getting treatment means you have an excellent chance of living a long, long life," I replied steadily, trying to sound hopeful. She absorbed my words and moved past them to the heart of what was really on her mind.

"I'm not afraid of dying, because I know I'll be with Jesus. I'm just afraid of *how* I would die."

I wanted to answer her with my body, to shelter her concern with great wings, like a mother bird over her nest. But she was already out on the limb, and now I had to help her find and trust her own wings. "I don't think dying hurts too much," I said, "because the nurses and doctors can give you lots of medicine to take away any pain. If you were to die, we would be right there, probably holding you, and it would be just like we passed you into the arms of Jesus."

"Shhh! Be quiet, Mommy!" she ordered as a bicyclist wheeled by us. We had opened up a treasure chest of rare secrets. She was not yet ready to publicize her find.

"I don't want to be the first in our family to die," she continued when the coast was clear, her voice more fervent than before.

"Any one of us could die first. Lauren or Leslie could be in an accident tomorrow and be killed. None of us knows the time when we will die. Only God knows."

I looked down at her face, her eyebrows knit, her eyes far away. She was visualizing her trip to the unknown, and she wanted the familiar to precede here. "Will Tucker be there when I get to heaven?"

Her question tore at my heart. I could picture our sweet, lovable pup greeting her at the gates of heaven with squirmy enthusiasm and endless kisses. I would have given anything to be able to promise this to her.

"I don't know, honey, but I know it will be a wonderful place. You'll feel happier being there than when you first saw Tucker after two weeks in the hospital. In fact, you'll be happier being there, I believe, than you are being with us."

The conversation halted while we entered the store to get

the milk. Kelly declined the Slushy. When we came out, we picked up where we had left off. I spoke to her about that which I knew, that which I surmised, and that which remained a mystery to me. And in the powerful line of trust that met in our clasped hands, she was eventually satisfied.

Arriving back home, she spotted her next-door neighbor playing on the swing set in the backyard. "Can I play with Caitlyn now?" she asked, letting go of my hand. We closed the treasure chest for the time being. I let her keep the key. There would be other days, I knew, when she would need it again.

The following week we made two separate trips to Philadelphia, these times to the Hospital of the University of Pennsylvania, adjacent to CHOP. We went for radiation simulation, a process of tattooing several pinhead-size dots at strategic points on Kelly's head to mark where the radiation would be focused. During these visits, Dr. Goldwein explained the process to us and reviewed the risks.

"She'll receive two doses four to six hours apart, Monday through Friday, for six straight weeks. During the second week, she'll receive what will be her first weekly dose of chemotherapy in addition to the radiation. The treatment can cause nausea and, within about 10 days, hair loss."

Dr. Goldwein told us that there could be long-term effects from radiation to the brain, beginning about a year after treatment and continuing up to five years or more. They could include stunted growth, hearing loss, learning problems, diminished IQ, and cataracts, to name just a few.

It was more than I could bear, but what choice did we have? I thought of Kelly's love of reading, her beautiful clear, sweet singing voice, her bright aptitude for learning. To see her appearance dramatically changed, and then have her gifts marred from the treatment as well, seemed more than cruel.

It was only four days until she and I would move to the Ronald McDonald House for five-day stints at a time. Because of the twice-daily radiation treatments, it simply wasn't feasible to go home each day. And so we arranged to stay in the weekend manager's suite Sunday night through Friday afternoon, then return home for the weekend.

After finishing supper the Friday before the start of radiation therapy, Rob loaded the girls in the car and took them for a short evening hike near a favorite creek of his. I stayed at home to get ready for our trip. From the window in the living room, I watched them pull out of the driveway and disappear down the road. I was so grateful for Rob's special gifts of doing fun things with the kids, even in the throes of his deep, agonizing concern for Kelly. In that rare moment of solitude, with the deep rose-golden sunlight stretching its long low rays into the living room, I knew I had heart preparations to make, as well. I grabbed two pillows off the sofa and sank, stomach down, onto the floor.

If it could have registered the intensity of my prayers over the years, the center of the living room floor would have shown a worn spot on the carpet. Tonight, however, the agony of my heart threatened to burn entirely through it.

I was silent for a while as I lay there. When I was in this spot, I did not even have to address God to bring him into the center of my thinking. This was *our* place, a consecrated rendezvous point established long ago, and so the moment I slumped to the floor, I felt I was already in his arms. I started to cry like a baby. "Is this *really* your will, to subject Kelly's precious head to the devastating effects of radiation? It seems so cruel, so devastating," I sobbed. "What about the beautiful voice you gave her, what about her love for reading, what about her ear for music? God, you can heal her! Why, oh why, won't you?"

It has always been the frustration of my impatient soul that God is not typically given to rapid-fire response or excessive feedback. "Maybe more people would love you if you talked more," I told him one night on a walk after Kelly, two-and-a-half years old at the time, had lost her teddy bear. For two nerve-wracking days we couldn't find him. I had been angry.

"You KNOW where her teddy is, and you're not helping us. You've seen how she hasn't been able to sleep well for two nights."

I had known God to give us special wisdom in helping us find both Lauren's teddy (buried under the snow on the road outside of church) and Leslie's stuffed kitty (buried inside the back of a toy truck) the same day they were lost, so I couldn't figure out why God wouldn't help us with Kelly's teddy. But I was frustrated over more than the teddy bear. I needed more response from God in general about life, assurances that this truly was a *relationship,* where both parties participate and *talk.*

I had come home that night, disheartened. Within seconds of my walking in the door, the phone rang. "Ello, dis iss Ahrridjannull Pizzuh," came the Italian voice on the other end.

"Original Pizza?" I said.

"Yez. We zink we found your liddull teddy bear."

Ecstatic, and sufficiently humbled in light of my remarks to God, I raced down to the pizza shop where we had posted a paper with a drawing of teddy on it. We had gotten pizza there the night we lost him. I hadn't recalled Kelly taking teddy in there, but I wasn't sure. Originally (ahrridjannully!) they told us they hadn't seen any such item in their restaurant. They assured us that they would have saved a stuffed animal if they had come across one.

It was Rob's idea to post the drawing, and, sure enough, someone who swept the floor that night vaguely recalled seeing a pink teddy. He was in the trash, only moments from being hauled away, when this woman saw my drawing and made the connection.

I took him from their hands and held him, clean and wet, to my heart. The pizza staff, standing in a group, their warm, dark eyes full of compassion, had washed him before I came. "Thank you, thank you!" I said. "You don't know how important this little guy is."

Much as I wrestled with him sometimes, I knew God's friendship well. I trusted him deeply. And so now, sprawled on the living room floor and swimming in tears, I needed desperately to hear from him. I pictured the radiation machine spewing forth its deadly rays onto Kelly's precious, vulnerable head. I saw it stripping her of life and vitality. I saw it—

Jesus Lover of My Soul. The hymn title came into my spirit, interrupting my thoughts. I knew the ring of God's voice in my spirit, his mysterious way of calling me to himself.

I got up off the floor and took a hymnbook from the piano. I found the hymn in the index, and it was familiar to me, but I had never memorized its text. Desperate for solace, I sat at the piano and began to sing:

Jesus, lover of my soul, let me to thy bosom fly,
While the nearer waters roll, while the tempest still is high.
Hide me, O my Savior, hide, till the storm of life is past;
Safe into the haven guide; O receive my soul at last . . .

I thought of Kelly lying under the radiation and included her in the sweet comfort of the words . . .

All my trust on thee is stayed, all my help from thee I bring;
Cover my defenseless head with the shadow of thy wing . . .

I choked on the last line, halting my voice as well as the accompaniment. Without God speaking another word, I knew this was the line he wanted me to see. He was calling me to trust in the sovereignty of his protective wing, to accept the power of that wing between Kelly's defenseless head and the deadly radiation rays. God had broken my defensive walls of mistrust, fear, and terror, and the shattered pieces came washing out of my system.

I felt the specific promise of his protection against her getting harmed by the radiation. That was all. No guarantees of anything else except for two things: light for the next step, and love for all of the journey. It was enough. Manna sufficient for the day.

Rob and I nearly needed to be physically pushed out the door the next night. "You two need some time alone together," came the words of Rob's mother. "Go see a movie, do *something*. We'll stay with the kids."

I had been emotionally joined at the hip with Kelly ever since her diagnosis. I didn't take well to the idea of going out on a date, or of even giving myself permission to have some kind of restorative recreation. What if something happened while I was gone? Would others know what to do? I deemed myself the indispensable caretaker, made a bed for myself in the garden of anxiety. Ma-Ma got her allies working for her, however. The children insisted we go, and so we made plans to see the summer hit, *Sister Act*.

Seated in the theater, I felt conspicuous in the middle of the casual, popcorn-eating crowd. Could people see what we had been through? Did it show on our faces? Our clothing? I felt strangely removed from the pre-movie banter—like an outsider looking in on a room full of laughter and levity. Could I ever be a part of this again?

I tried hard to push away the scary thoughts of radiation. Once the movie started I was able to let the anxiety go. Gradually, I began to relax—and even smile.

That night in the darkness of our bedroom, we stared up at the ceiling. The room, though quiet to the ear, seemed filled with the noisy energy of our inner thoughts. The movie had been a pleasant respite. But now, the anxiety was back. Two more nights in this bed, and then Philadelphia for most of the rest of the summer.

Rob reached for my hand. For a moment he infused warmth into my anxiety-ridden body. We talked about how emotionally depleted our lives had become, about how selfish and irreverent the idea of making love felt to both of us in the middle of such severe suffering for one of our children.

We prayed briefly. Our entire beings throughout the past month were perpetually God-poised and anchored in agonizing supplication. We didn't usually say more than a few short strands of words out loud. This night Rob stopped in the middle of one. "You know," he said thoughtfully, "I think making love in the midst of all this wouldn't be irreverent; it'd be a sign of trust in God, don't you think?"

It was a permission-giving thought and a redefining moment in our journey.

12.

We left for Philadelphia on Monday morning, July 20th, at 5:30 a.m. We had allowed extra time for heavy traffic on the Schuylkill and were glad we did. "I appreciate you guys coming along," I told Lauren and Leslie as we ground to a halt behind full lanes of traffic at the turnpike exit toll booths. "It makes it so much easier to go through this when you have support and extra help."

Sleepily propped up against each other like three fallen dominoes, they groaned a halfhearted response. I smiled at them. Okay, so this wasn't exactly a picnic. I knew it as well as they. Still, I was grateful. The encouragement they provided Kelly was incomparable to anything Rob or I could give her.

We arrived early at the Hospital of the University of Pennsylvania, adjacent to CHOP, and gave our car to the valet parking attendant. We registered at the desk in the radiation therapy clinic and took seats in the waiting area. Kelly and the girls opened a tote bag of games and drawing items I had gathered and busily occupied themselves. Rob picked up a magazine.

I studied the people around us. I wondered which ones were here for radiation and which were family members supporting them. My eyes fell on the back of the head of a young boy about Kelly's size. Appearing lighter on his dark skin was the familiar zipper-like pattern of stitches that Kelly had.

He stood up to get a different magazine. When he turned around, I read his T-shirt: *What a Mighty God We Serve.* It had to be the same boy. I had to make sure. "Excuse me," I said to the woman beside him. "I think I saw you in ICU at CHOP the day after my daughter had brain surgery. She had a brain tumor removed. Is—is that what your son had?" I was uncharacteristically forward, but I was anxious to know someone going through what we were, so I took the chance.

Her face brightened immediately. "Yes, he had a brain tumor removed, too. Is today your first day of radiation also?"

"Yes. We're on a treatment schedule for two times a day."

"You are? So are we."

I liked her immediately. And I liked that I had a potential friend. "My name's Lisa. I really love the message on your son's T-shirt. It's a good reminder to me this morning."

"I'm Cindy, and I know just what you mean."

In a few short minutes we had covered miles of common ground, down to the very similar elements of our Christian faith. She introduced me to her four children, and I introduced them to my family. Christopher, her seven-year-old son, and Kelly seemed particularly happy to meet each other.

For the glory of God. I had pictured God taking us through all this so that somehow others might come to know him. Now I was seeing a new way of glorifying God. Two women and two children in the Lord, providing rich comfort and support for each other, could also bring him glory in the midst of painful circumstances. God's purposes are not only for others, but also for us.

"Christopher King, Kelly Bair," came the receptionist's voice. Cindy and I walked back the hall with the kids. A jovial man named Max joked with us and diffused the incredible intensity of the moment. A calm, loving woman named Helen worked with him.

The kids had been prepared. Chris went first. He was finished in about five minutes.

"Kelly, your turn," Max said, leading her into the radiation room.

It was over painlessly and quickly enough. Back in the waiting area, Kelly announced to Lauren, "It smelled like a skunk in that room!" One down. Only 59 more treatments to go.

We said good-bye to the Kings, who drove to their home in nearby Media, and then we got in our car to travel the several blocks to the Ronald McDonald House. "You'll like this place," Rob said. "It's beautiful inside and very homey."

After we registered at the desk, Rob led us to the top of the steps on the second floor and put the key into the latch. He opened the door and my mouth fell open. "This is *gorgeous,*" I said, stopping in my tracks to take it all in.

The room looked like some sort of presidential suite. Spacious with a high ceiling, the suite's pale blue walls were set off by ornate strips of molding, trimmed in off-white. A large fireplace with a mirror on top was the central focus of the room, which also featured huge, floor-to-ceiling windows outfitted with shutters. An adjacent room with table and chairs led into a large, newly remodeled bathroom.

"Are you sure we're in the right room?" I asked incredulously.

"It's much fancier than the room I stayed in," Rob said, "but they like to have oncology families in here. They usually come for Monday through Friday treatment, and then they leave. Then the weekend manager can stay here over the weekend."

We set up three cots for the girls in the ample space around the double bed and unpacked our suitcases. After that we carried food items downstairs to the kitchen where we put them in a designated storage cabinet.

Cheerful and well-equipped, the kitchen/dining/sitting area was the most active place in the House. Simultaneously, at just about any given moment, people were eating, watching TV, playing complimentary games of PAC Man on a machine donated to the place, or watching kids in the play corner or outside in the yard. Kelly was fascinated watching her sisters play PAC Man and wanted to learn how to do it herself.

After our brief tour, we went upstairs to rest. Soon our intercom system clicked on. "Hello?" came a pleasant voice.

"Yes?" Rob answered.

"There's a group going over to Veteran's Stadium tonight to see the Phillies. We have five extra tickets. Would you like to go?"

We all looked at each other, not knowing how to respond to this gracious hospitality. "Uh, yes," Rob finally said. "That would be wonderful. We'd enjoy that."

"Okay, great. We leave at 7:00 from the side parking lot. See you then."

We had just settled back into our beds to relax when Kelly suddenly groaned in a manner with which I had become all too familiar. I jumped up and ran to grab a small basin—just in time. She vomited forcefully into it.

My heart sank. I knew cranial radiation could cause nausea, but I didn't realize it would hit this abruptly or this violently. She settled back into her bed and spent the next four hours sleeping and getting sick.

Soon it was time for the second radiation treatment of the day. "Now we have to take her back to repeat all this," I complained to Rob. "I hate to waken her. What if she's sick like this the whole summer?"

We had no choice but to rouse her. Rob carried her the whole way. Back in the radiation therapy room, Cindy King was sitting alone with Chris. He was holding a basin in his lap. "He's sick, too?" I asked sympathetically.

"Yes," she said, "several times."

I read in Cindy's face all the feelings I felt—the weariness, the fear, the motherly concern mixed with the hatred for this treatment. We ministered to each other with eyes that held great tanks of empathy, arms that occasionally soothed each other's shoulders.

"We have some medicine that can help the vomiting," Dr.

Goldwein assured me. "We will keep tabs on Kelly all the way through the treatment, so keep me informed of your concerns."

That night Rob went with Lauren and Leslie to the Phillies game while Kelly and I stayed back in the room. Within a few days, the medicine had taken care of the vomiting almost entirely, although Kelly didn't feel well most of the time and often ate only a meager 150 calories in a day. I agonized about what to feed her, worried that starvation would kill her, if not the cancer.

Thursday evening we said good-bye to Rob and Lauren and Leslie. Rob had to go to work, and the girls were missing their friends and losing interest in the activities available to them. "We'll see you tomorrow night," I said, kissing them all good-bye. That evening and the next morning, Kelly wrote in her journal, sounding out most of her words and occasionally asking me to spell others:

July 23, 1992

It is 7:04 in the evening, I feel a little lonly and a little sad, but I thingk I can manage it throw this last day of being in Philadelphia. Nexs week I start chemotherapy. It is not going to be much fun but I will make it be fun. Radiatiln is hard to get throw, too, But I will make that fun too. It was a very boring day because it was raining the hole entire day. I'm a little nervous abowt starting chemotherapy because it is very boring. I dindin't even get sike (1) time today. tomorrow I go home and see my honny sweetie Tucker.

July 24, 1992

It is 9:57 in the morning, I still feel a little lonly and sad. I am going home today after my last treatment for the week. I feel very good that I am going home, Now Philadelphia seems to be my home, but it rely isant. today was a perety normal day, waking up going to treatment and going bake to the ronold McDonld House. today at treatment I got to eat a donute, it tasted rely good too.

A TABLE FOR TWO

Our weekend at home was breathlessly short. We had time for little else other than doing laundry, repacking food supplies, checking in with the family, going to church, and then heading back to Philadelphia Sunday evening.

It was raining the night we returned to the city for week number two of treatment. This time the rest of the family remained at home. We would be joined by Linda, a friend from Virginia, who graciously offered to stay with us for the week.

As usual, Kelly was in no mood to be awakened for her first treatment on Monday morning. Getting the required anti-nausea medicine into her in the morning, when she didn't feel well to begin with, was difficult. I had taken to carrying her to the car and through the hospital corridors for most of her appointments, particularly the ones early in the day. She simply felt too weak and sick to move on her own.

Her eating by this point had fallen below sustenance level, and most of what she did ingest occurred late in the day, never in the morning. When she was weighed after one of her treatments, she had dropped to a new low—16 pounds below her normal weight. It became the agonizing focus of every day to try to provide foods that would appeal to her. Often she would ask for spaghetti or a doughnut. I would jump at the chance to make whatever she requested, only to find her unable to eat more than a bite or two. I fed her slightest food whims, no matter how unhealthy they were. To feed her nutritionally, or at designated mealtimes, was simply out of the question. The focus, unhappily, became calories—any kind—for survival.

Kelly had grown very fond of playing PAC Man, and, since she loved it so much, I would let her play during mealtimes, then try to slip in a spoonful of something while she was concentrating on the game. This worked better than making her sit at the table, where staring at the food turned her stomach.

By Tuesday of that week, I had to carry Kelly over to CHOP to receive her first chemotherapy, a shot of vincristine. I attempted to teach her a simple breathing technique I had learned prior to childbirth to help her relax with the pain of the injection. She tried it, and it seemed to help. She didn't protest when the needle went into her arm.

"That's all there is to it?" I asked the nurse after the few seconds it took.

"That's all," she said, smiling.

"Kelly, this won't be so bad," I said. She smiled, proud that she had weathered the shot without complaint. Dr. Janss came to get Kelly to examine her. This affectionate woman had come to be a source of great cheer to us. Her smile and caring enthusiasm did wonders for our emotions. Her loving manner transcended the harsh devastation of the treatment in ways that kept our dim fires of hope from going out. We looked forward to seeing her and treasured her encouraging touch.

Back at the House, I met a woman whose son was in the hospital with severe liver problems. A Jewish cantor, she played guitar and sang well. One evening my friend Linda, with whom I had often worked in music, and I joined her in the living room where there was a piano. "Are there some Psalms we could sing together?" I asked her. "I know two in Hebrew, although my Hebrew isn't very good. How 'bout 'Hiney Mah Tov?'"

The woman immediately began to strum her guitar and sing it, and Linda joined her on the flute. I played the chords on the piano, and, for a few precious moments, we transcended our weariness and faith differences with the joy of our God and his gift of music. While we sang the Hebrew, the English translation played in my mind: *Behold, how good and pleasant it is for brethren to dwell together in unity . . .*

There was a unique spirit of unity among the parents at the House. Knit together by the common cord of suffering, we had become family. In spite of that, I was still totally surprised when on Thursday evening, July 30th, Kelly and I and Rob, who had joined us for the night, were summoned downstairs.

We turned the corner into the kitchen and suddenly saw balloons and streamers, kids and parents gathered around a long table, singing, "Happy birthday to you! Happy birthday to you! Happy birthday, dear Kelly, happy birthday to you!"

The exuberant spirit of the song warmed our hearts. Even if we didn't have what it took to make our own celebration, these people were going to see to it that we didn't drown in our sorrow. Kelly opened gifts from many families, some of whom were strapped financially with medical bills. Yet they still gave a gift to a child they hardly knew. There were coloring books, necklaces, crayons, markers, books, and a huge cake. Kelly was delighted. She even ate a small piece of cake.

In bed that night, my heart was warmed deeply by the graciousness of those around us. I watched the Chestnut Street traffic split and scramble the patterns of soft, grayish-blue streetlight on the walls and ceiling of our room. Philadelphia, the city of brotherly love, had stretched out its arms to us. It was beginning to feel a little like home.

13.

The following Tuesday during our visit to the clinic, the nurse tried twice to get Kelly's veins to receive the injection but could not succeed. Kelly was beginning to lose her calm. "I'm sorry, Kelly," she said. "I only try twice, and then I send for someone else. I'm going to get another nurse to try, okay?"

The second nurse failed twice, as well. By this time, Kelly was whimpering. Dr. Janss came in. "Let's not try anymore. This happened sooner than I thought it would, but it is expected nevertheless. Chemo patients' veins often collapse and can't be used for the injections. It's much simpler and easier for the patient to have an infusaport or Broviac put in, so it's time to think about which one would be easier for you both.

"These are permanent attachments to one of the main arteries to the heart. With the Broviac, the apparatus is all outside the skin, so shots are given through the tubing. But you have to clean it everyday, and it's more work for the parents. You also cannot get it wet.

"The infusaport is embedded under the skin, so while she'd still feel the prick initially, the skin toughens up over time. It would be nicer since she'd be able to go swimming. But it's your choice. You decide whichever is best for you."

Rob and I discussed the pros and cons, then thought of

Tucker and his jumping up on Kelly. "I'd hate to have him rip it out," I said.

Once we agreed on the infusaport, surgery was set for August 4th of the following week. "I cannot guarantee how long it will last," the surgeon said. "I've had some last a week. Others have lasted a year. Recently I had to replace one two weeks before the boy finished his entire cycle of chemotherapy." His words, though necessary and informative, disheartened me.

We returned to our room that afternoon, thoroughly tired. For one week only we had been moved to a regular room with a huge, king-sized bed in the center of it. Comfortably sprawled on the bed, I immersed myself in writing a letter. I thought Kelly was coloring.

"Mommy," she said, lying on her stomach with her knees bent and ankles bouncing off each other rhythmically. "What does 'thirty percent sur-*vivval* rate' mean?"

I looked up with a start. *Oh, no.* I hadn't meant for her to see those pamphlets. Laying pen and paper aside, I sighed with resignation and looked sympathetically at her face. My eyes lingered on the widening part in her hair. For several days now her blonde, shoulder-length hair had been coming out in clumps. By tomorrow, I guessed mournfully, all of it would be gone.

Remember the wing, I ordered my sinking heart, recalling God's promise to me during prayer the weekend before we began the radiation. "C'mere, kiddo," I said, turning on my side and patting a spot on the bed for Kelly to nestle under my arm. We sank down into the pillows and drew close. I nuzzled her thinning hair and kissed the sweet warmth of her head. I had let her keep the key to the treasure chest, and now it was open again.

I explained the term as simply as I could. Then, very naturally, she asked about heaven. Like two friends camped out for an evening under the stars, we began to dream of it out loud to each other, to shiver and giggle as we stretched our collective imagination into eternal infinity. Gradually, as the sun dipped behind city buildings, the room began to darken cozily—*like being covered with the shadow of God's wing,* I thought.

"Oh Mom," Kelly whispered in the reverent wonder of the moment. "I can't wait to go to heaven."

We were no longer mother and daughter, but two children resting together in the palm of God's hand—where sorrow shrivels and hope springs a thousand fountains. "Neither can I," I said longingly. "Neither can I."

The next morning I woke Kelly, only to find her pillow covered with loose hair. I got her up and gave her the required medicine, then changed the bandage on an infected part of her incision that was late in healing, due to the radiation.

"We're late for treatment, honey. We've got to step on it." I reached for her brush and attempted to remove the loose strands that hung below her hairline. But her hair had completely lost its rootedness. I pulled the waste can over and literally brushed almost all the hair off her head.

After watching several thick clumps of hair fall into the waste can, Kelly ran to the mirror. "I look like an alien," she said, bursting into tears.

The dreaded reality had arrived, and there was no time to ponder it. "We've got to go," I said sympathetically. "I wish, too, this wouldn't have to be a part of your treatment, but, unfortunately, neither you nor I can do anything about it."

While we had previously had a wig custom-made for her, the radiation had stalled the healing process in Kelly's incision, so she couldn't wear it. I gave her a bright pink safari hat—the only one I could find ahead of time to prepare for this awful moment. She was pale, thin, and now shorn of her crowning glory. At the hospital she walked past Helen without even a response to her morning greeting. We were both irritable and depressed.

Five minutes later Kelly emerged smiling. I stared in disbelief. "What happened in there?"

"Helen told me just to be glad it's not two weeks before my

wedding day," she said, laughing. "Oh, Mommy, look what she gave me!" She opened up a small box and pulled out a beautiful flowered, silk ponytail scrunchie. "Isn't it pretty? She said it's for when my hair grows back."

I could have kissed Helen.

I happened to see Kelly's journal lying open the next morning. Her latest entry was terse, and the rest of the page was covered with angry scribbles: *I lost my hair on Agust 6, 1992 it is very miserabl, and very bothering, and I rely hate it.*

After treatment the next afternoon, a clear and sunny one in early August, Kelly and I left for Stone Harbor, New Jersey. We were going to the beach home of a friend who graciously lent us his place until we could link up with my extended family the next day in nearby Avalon. He understood what we were going through—his wife had a brain tumor, too. "Just think, Kelly," I said triumphantly. "You're halfway through radiation! Thirty treatments down, 30 to go!"

With 50 or so miles behind us, the grip of treatment and city living loosening its hold on us with every mile, we began to feel lighter and more relaxed at the prospect of the beach. We would be staying for two days only, but we were determined to make it feel like two weeks.

It was suppertime when we pulled into Stone Harbor. We easily located the house offered to us and proceeded to park. "Oh, Mommy, please . . . *please* can we go to the beach before we do anything else?" Kelly asked at the first sign of sand and water.

I needed no urging. It was 5:30 p.m., and the beach was fairly deserted. We stepped onto the sand and gulped in the delicious air—free of fumes, medicine, and disinfectants. The low evening sunlight, bathing the beach and water in soft pinks and golds, poured vibrant color back into our hospital-fatigued senses.

Kelly went off on her own to look for shells, one hand holding onto her pink hat while the wind played butler and tugged underneath its brim as if to say, "May I take this, please? We are delighted to have you. Please make yourself at home."

"This is the best day of my life!" Kelly shouted exuberantly from the water's edge where she twirled around to take in the panorama of sea and sky, then stooped to pick up an array of tiny shells. "I want it to last forever!"

We had entered nature's door, and her lavish hospitality expertly mended our frayed spirits. We were being healed, and one of the sure signs for Kelly was the restoration of hunger. "Can we eat supper soon?" she asked after we had walked a good distance along the shoreline and gathered many shells. Always looking for ways to nourish her, I was prepared for the moment and handed her a sweet, ripe nectarine I had in my pocket.

"Daddy and your sisters should be here soon," I said. "Let's try to find something for them, too, in case they haven't eaten." We went back to the car, then drove to a little store in town and bought a hot, fresh-roasted chicken, a bag of frozen peas, a quart of milk, and a box of doughnuts. Back at the house I cooked the peas and served Kelly a spoonful of them on a plate with a few cut-up pieces of chicken and a tiny glass of milk.

Kelly ate ravenously, exclaiming over the taste of the food and about how hungry she was. I filled her plate again, then again, and yet another time. I watched in disbelief as she finished her meal by polishing off not one, but two, whole doughnuts and two more glasses of milk. My mother's heart took wings at this small triumph—the first whole meal Kelly had eaten in three weeks.

Shortly, Rob pulled into the driveway with the girls. I had pleaded with them over the phone to be encouraging about Kelly's baldness, which they had not yet seen. We all hugged each other, then Rob, Leslie, and Lauren stood back to check out Kelly's new look.

"You *do* look good," Rob said admiringly, acknowledging that, even at the age of seven, his youngest daughter had acquired a bit of vanity.

"Kelly, you look like one of those models who purposely

shaves her head to look fashionable," Lauren said, smiling. She gave a thumbs up, and Kelly grinned.

"You look different, that's for sure," Leslie said. "But you have a nice head, and you look cute."

"Kelly, we made you a tape," the girls said excitedly. "Wanna hear it?"

She was thrilled to have them around again, and the energy of their support lifted her spirits even higher. Soon we were all gathered around a miniature tape recorder, listening to Tucker howl with the fire siren at home, followed by a series of radio "oldies" produced on the trip down to the beach, humorously narrated by the three of them just for Kelly's enjoyment. She laughed heartily at this original gift.

After everyone finished off the chicken, the peas, and the doughnuts, we went out on the deck and watched the moon, strikingly brilliant over the ocean. The rhythm of the waves hushed our conversation and lulled us into deep rest.

"It's been so long since I've felt this 'together' and this peaceful," Rob said, soaking up the beauty and the sound. "I wish we could stay here forever."

We moved back into the house, and, although we had planned to sleep in the beds, we missed each other too much to separate. It was our chance to tie together the threads of family life which had become loose and disheveled over these last few months. We gathered pillows and blankets from the car and stretched out in the center of the living room floor. Without a word, someone started our traditional tickling chain, each of us softly stoking the back, arms, legs, or feet of the person next to us. We each spoke simple sentences of thanksgiving to God, then drifted off, content.

14.

When the day of surgery arrived to install Kelly's infusaport, her previous surgical experience had taken the bite out of her anxiety. But Rob and I weren't as relaxed. Knowing what she would endure in the day was a grueling order.

First, she would receive her morning dose of radiation, then be taken to surgery, after which, upon waking from full anesthesia, she would receive her first dose of vincristine through her new infusaport. Later, she would be wheeled to radiation for her second afternoon treatment.

"Can a child take all this in one day?" I asked Rob. But she did, and, by evening, back in bed in our beautiful suite at the Ronald McDonald House, she had only a small bandage over her incision and a slightly irritable disposition to show for it.

Midweek, my brother's wife brought Lauren and Leslie up from the shore in Avalon to be with us. During the afternoon she took them shopping for school clothes. Within two days Kelly felt well enough to go, too, so we loaded her up in Ann's little convertible and whisked her off to the King of Prussia shopping mall.

Shopping was Kelly's favorite diversion, even if it was only a short browse through one of the hospital gift shops. Tonight's mission, however, was hats. My sister-in-law, with her stylish fashion sense, had a vision for what she wanted to find for Kelly, so we let her lead.

Floppy, white hats with flowers on them had only begun to penetrate the market, but, by evening's end, Kelly owned an adorable white hat with a navy blue-and-white-checked lining that turned up in the front and sported a big yellow daisy. It was charming on her. When I looked at her wearing it I suddenly felt a spirit of overcoming, of joy in the middle of suffering. The hat brought a beautiful new look, as well as ease and cool comfort in its wearing. We put away the wig we had made without too much further thought.

Kelly's shots of vincristine brought on muscular aches and pains and a suppression of her immunity system, as side effects. One night she complained of difficulty urinating. By morning, she was in severe pain. I knelt with her while she sat on the toilet crying loudly, "I can't go! It hurts too much!" But she had to go—desperately. And with her attempt to do so, she let out a piercing scream, her legs kicking frantically, her eyes full of panic.

It was too much for her—and for me. I pictured the entire next year overrun with infections. I resented every ounce of toxic, cancer-killing treatment for invading and debilitating Kelly's body. Her scream plumbed the depths of my stored-up anger over this entire ordeal. A scathing internal scream of my own, which I held back from exploding audibly, rose up and silently lashed out with hers.

My eyes were wide with desperation as I tried to calm her while she flailed on the toilet. I gritted my teeth and pounded bitterly on God's heart. *How much more do we have to take? Is this your good pleasure to inflict even more pain in this child's life? My eyes burned with tears as Kelly kept screaming. You HAVE to help her! and NOW! I DEMAND that you help her!*

Was it a miracle? I didn't know. I was too frayed inside to tell. But within a few moments, Kelly quieted down. At her radiation treatment that afternoon the doctors put her on an antibiotic which seemed to help within a couple of hours.

The next night we headed back to the shore again and milked our last evening there for all it was worth. We went home Saturday, only to return to Philadelphia the next day. It was a lot of driving, but the emotional replenishment we received made it worthwhile. Our last morning at the shore, Kelly wrote this letter:

August 15, 1992
Dear tucker,

I hope Ma-Ma has been taking good care of you! Were you eating well wiall I was gone? I hope so! Did you go to the bathrom in the hous yet? I hope not! We had a great time at the bech . . . I rely did wish you could come alog with us! I missed you a lot! did you miss me? So how are the newts? are thay eating well too? I hope so!

We went out to a seafood restaurant for dinner last night. it was rely fun. I got a delicious platter of shrimp. then we went bake to the house and watched a movie. This morning I played with Sarah. It also rained dogs and cats today. I got a new T-shirt, swet pants and a book, it was rely fun going shoping!

Love,
you'r sister Kelly

By week five of our stay in Philadelphia, we began to feel the thrill of light at the end of the tunnel. We counted down the remaining treatments . . . 20, 19, 18 . . .

We were also taking a more active role in the House these days. No longer the rookies, we spent several evenings helping Teri, the weekend manager, cook meals for the House. She came over voluntarily once or twice a week to prepare supper for everyone, and I loved helping her. She had a real flair for food presentation and saw to it that each meal was nutritious and appealing.

She taught me how to score cucumbers with a fork, giving the slices a flower-like look, and to cut red and green peppers in long thin strips to beautify salads. I enjoyed her friendship immensely, and the time we spent preparing food became a precious diversion for me. Kelly worked nearby, honing her skill at the PAC Man machine.

I was deeply restored by looking at the colorful beauty of fresh vegetables and the carefully marinated and grilled roast Teri had shopped for and lovingly prepared. With the medical emergency and geographic scrambling of everything else in our lives, our eating had too often been hurried and of fast-food quality. Teri's simple and attractive offerings took on meaning which transcended their nutritional quality.

As our gift to the House our last week there, Lauren and Leslie helped me prepare an evening meal for everyone. We made three 9 x 12 pans full of a crunchy chicken casserole, cleaned several pounds of fresh green beans and carrots, scrubbed over 30 potatoes and wrapped them in aluminum foil, and made four dozen chocolate cream cheese cupcakes. It took all day between our radiation appointments, but I was so glad to return something small to the place that extended so much warm hospitality to us.

As I lay in bed beside Kelly the night before her last day of treatment, I could hardly believe she had only two more treatments to go, or that this would be our last night in our presidential-like suite. Next week there would be people like us, now on the waiting list, who would occupy this room—people whose futures were precarious, whose love for their children was breaking their hearts.

God, bless this room, I whispered in the darkness. *May all who stay here know your sufficiency in their need. Thank you for your care through all the people who have reached out to help us, and for all those with bulging wallets and giving hearts who laid the groundwork for and keep supporting this wonderful House.*

Thank you for enlarging my heart toward those who suffer physically, and toward you. I've complained a lot, Lord. But I can testify to all that you haven't yet been untrue to your word. I haven't always realized it at the time, but you've been wonderfully gracious and present to us.

I laid my hand on Kelly's forehead. *And now, for this precious child, give her strength for the days ahead as she enters second grade soon and has to deal with her looks, as well as absences for chemotherapy and the ever-present threat of infections. Be with her, God. Give her peace.*

15.

"Expect that your classmates will be curious about you," I told Kelly as I helped her into her shorts on the opening day of school. "You'd be curious, too, if one of your friends had lost all their hair. Some might not even recognize you, remember, since you've lost a lot of weight. Just give them time. Answer their questions as simply as you can. After a while they'll get used to you."

We had covered everything a dozen times: "If you feel tired or sick, just tell Mrs. Bear. I've already talked with her, and she'll help you in every way she can. The nurse has all your medicines and knows to expect you sometimes . . .

"If you're not hungry at lunchtime, ask if you can eat part of your lunch during recess in your room . . .

"Don't forget to drink . . .

"Don't worry about doing everything everybody else does in gym class or at recess. Rest when you need to. Leslie's down the hall in sixth grade if you need her for anything."

"Mom, I know, I know. You've told me a hundred times!" Terribly thin and pale, Kelly looked as if her shorts were wearing her. She had already vomited that morning, but I assumed it was due to anxiety. I opted to drive her to school the first week, just to give her more time to get going and, possibly, to eat something. This morning she could eat nothing.

I waited by the phone all day, expecting a call. There was none. When I went to her classroom to pick her up, she looked content, and Mrs. Bear reported that the day had gone well.

"How did it go?" I asked Kelly, studying her face intently.

"Good," she said, smiling a little.

"Did anyone tease you about your hair?"

"No."

"Did they ask questions about it?"

"Yes," she answered, sighing wearily. "Mommy, I'm tired." She laid her head back on the seat of the car while we waited for Leslie to come. I didn't press further.

When we got home I pulled her squashed, barely picked-at lunch from her book bag. "Kelly, is this all you ate?"

"I wasn't hungry. It makes me feel sick to eat in the cafeteria. And everyone rushes." She slumped onto the sofa. "Sesame Street" began to relax her. And before long, she requested food.

Rob and I agreed with Mrs. Bear that it would be helpful to talk to Kelly's class about her illness. So, with Kelly's permission, I went on the third day of school. Kelly wanted to be absent from the room while I talked, so she went to the nurse.

Mrs. Bear introduced me. I smiled before 22 sets of inquisitive, seven-year-old eyes. "How many of you have noticed anything different about Kelly this year?" I began.

Three hands shot up. I acknowledged a little girl in the far corner. "Kelly wears hats more often," she responded thoughtfully.

Another boy vigorously waved his raised hand. "I think she has a line up the back of her neck."

"I—I'm not sure," came the soft voice of another little girl, "but I don't think she has any hair."

"Well, you're all exactly right, and I want to tell you why. In June, at the end of first grade, Kelly got very sick. And the doctors found that she had what's called a brain tumor." I scanned their attentive faces carefully as I proceeded. "Because tumors can make you very sick, Kelly had to have it removed in surgery. The doctors gave her lots of medicine to make her sleep so she didn't feel anything when they took it out, but the line up the back of her neck is where the incision was made."

One little girl raised her hand. "My mommy told me about this."

"Good," I said. "I'm glad some of you have already heard about it. Well, when the doctors took the tumor out, they found out that it was cancerous. Have any of you ever heard of cancer?"

One boy raised his hand. "I think you catch it from smoking."

"Well, smoking can sometimes cause certain kinds of cancer. But there are other kinds of cancer, too, not caused by smoking, and Kelly has one of those other kinds. It's very important that you all understand that you cannot 'catch' this from Kelly. No one catches cancer from another person. It's not like a cold or the chickenpox where, if one person has it, another might get it." I hesitated, trying to choose words that would inform, not create anxiety. "In fact, children hardly ever get cancer. It's very rare. But sometimes they do get it, and so, if they do, the doctors have to give them special kinds of treatment and medicines called 'chemotherapy' to try to keep any tumors from coming back.

"The problem is that the treatment and medicines make your hair fall out, so that's why Kelly's bald. Her hair will grow back, but probably not for a year—when she's all done taking her medicine."

The children didn't appear to be confused, so I continued. "To get some of this medicine, Kelly will need to stay in the hospital for a few days every now and then, so you may notice that she's absent a lot of days this year. And sometimes she just may not feel very good and might need to go to the nurse to rest for a little.

"I thought I'd come today in case you were wondering what was wrong with her and were afraid to ask. Do any of you have any more questions about it?" Apparently they were satisfied.

"Kelly's down at the nurse right now because she felt a little embarrassed to have us all talking about her. But she did tell me that you can ask her questions later if you want to, and she'll be glad to talk about it with you."

Kelly eventually asked to start riding the bus to school. One afternoon Leslie came home and reported that an older boy had lifted up Kelly's hat in the back and screamed, "Ooooh! This is the grossest thing I've ever seen!"

My heart was crushed. "Did you say anything to him?"

"I asked him how he would feel if he'd had brain surgery and someone did that to him," Leslie said, still fuming at the thought of him.

"It's okay, Mom," Kelly said from her reclining position on the sofa.

"Kelly, it's not gross looking," I said. "It's maybe a creepy thought for him to think of having an incision in his head."

"I know," Kelly said.

Our doctors in Philadelphia arranged for Kelly to receive blood checks and to take her outpatient shots of vincristine at Hershey Medical Center. Dr. Pamelyn Close, formerly from CHOP and well-acquainted with the treatment protocol there, would supervise her case.

"They want Kelly's first two inpatient hospitalizations at CHOP so they can monitor how she responds. After that, they're willing to let her receive them here," Dr. Close informed me. "I'll be in close touch with them through her entire treatment." She smiled warmly. "Welcome. We're glad to have you here."

Sunday night, October 11th, I was not in a good mood. It was the night before Kelly's and my trip to Philadelphia for her first inpatient chemotherapy. I had a bad cold, and Rob and I had had a misunderstanding. We sat in the family room trying to work through it.

"I guess I'm just uptight," I said, dabbing a tissue to my pooling eyes. "Okay, if the truth be known, I'm scared. I don't know what to expect from this, and I don't really want to go alone. I'm tired of our being separated as a family, and I hate all this treatment! I'm sick of it and what it's doing to her."

Rob listened sympathetically. I knew he wished he could go with me. It wasn't easy for him to keep his job going, to try to hold the house together, and to feel so concerned about us and what we were going through. He put his arms around me.

"And I'm sick of all these insurance forms," I said, getting it all out while there was a listening ear. "I don't even understand them. We're getting billed from four hospitals—outpatient and inpatient separately—and several doctor's offices. I'm drowning in all the paper."

He didn't try to solve the situation. It couldn't be done.

Monday, October 12th, we left for Philadelphia for a radiation follow-up examination. We would spend the night with our friends Jeff and Donna, then return to CHOP early the next day to be admitted for Kelly's first inpatient chemotherapy.

Jeff, a pastor, was home when we arrived. He had set the table and was working on supper. Soon Donna arrived, and gradually, as the evening wore on, my irritability unraveled in their gracious presence.

Jeff left to go to a meeting, and, while I took Kelly upstairs to get ready for bed, Donna went into the kitchen to make some tea. "Mommy, can I have some tea, too?" Kelly asked, lingering on the staircase.

Donna overheard her. "Sure, Kelly. Get your pajamas on and we'll have a little tea party."

It was pure and simple fellowship when the three of us in our cozy pajamas settled together on the sofa for tea and cookies. We talked and giggled like friends at a sleepover, and I felt sweet joy and contentment flow back into my veins.

The next day held a blood test and a complex kidney study to determine Kelly's capacity to process the chemotherapy. She also received an audiogram to determine her base hearing level. The drugs would be harsh, and hearing as well as kidney function could be affected. She would be monitored carefully. Finally, in the early evening, we were admitted and led to a room on the oncology floor.

There on her bed was a beautiful bouquet of flowers.

"Well aren't you lucky?" the nurse said. "I've never heard of anyone getting flowers in the hospital *before* they were admitted!" Our hearts melted as we read the words on the card: "We're with you all the way. We love you—Rob, Lauren, and Leslie."

Through her infusaport Kelly was hooked up to an IV and began to receive extensive hydration. "We have to make sure she's got enough fluid in her to handle the chemo," the nurse explained. "We'll be hydrating her for several hours, after which she'll receive the cisplatinum during the night. Then, she'll need to be hydrated for another 16 hours.

"Kelly, I need you to pee in the plastic white hat in the bathroom every time you go, okay?" Then the nurse gave her some other chemo pills. We watched a little TV and decided to call it a night.

We were not exactly rested by morning. With all the hydration, Kelly had to go to the bathroom every two hours. But her chemo was over, and she felt fine.

Initially she wanted to go to the playroom. But by late afternoon, the vitality-draining medicine began to take its toll. Not interested in food or much activity, Kelly stayed in bed most of the evening. The family-life specialist on the floor, a perky blonde with a heart for children and fun brought games and books from the playroom.

We were sent home the next morning with several doses of an anti-nausea drug, as well as instructions to buy magnesium tablets. "The cisplatinum causes the kidneys to spew out magnesium, so she'll need to take pills to replace it four times daily," the discharge nurse explained.

This was not a pleasant chore with the anti-nausea drugs

and antibiotics she already had to take. I couldn't imagine
adding more pills to our daily routine. Often Kelly would take
them readily, but just as often, it seemed, she balked and
moaned, staring for minutes on end—with her forehead
pressed into the palm of her hand—at a pill and a small glass
of water. And none of these pills were tiny. Some looked like
horse pills. We split them up into pieces, making it seem like
even more pills to take.

In early November Kelly began a mysterious pattern of early
morning vomiting, all too familiar to us. I called Dr. Close, my
voice on edge. "She's manifesting the very same symptoms she
did right before diagnosis."

"Bring her in tomorrow morning, and I'll try to contact
CHOP to see what they recommend."

That night fear set in and threatened to strangle us. Rob and
I took an evening walk. "What if it's grown back?" I asked,
choking up.

He was every bit as frightened as I. "I can't imagine how
aggressive this cancer must be if it has grown this fast." We
held hands, cried, and tried to steady ourselves.

When we returned home, I tried to occupy my mind by
cleaning up the kitchen counter, sorting through junk mail, cat-
alogs, and various other papers lying around. Underneath the
mess, I found a note from Kelly, scrawled in big letters and decorated with a heart:

For the Bible says, "Trust in the Lord you God!"
To: my famaliey—Leslie, Lauren, Lisa, Rob and to my dog tucker

The results of an emergency MRI scan the next day were
negative.

16.

November 3, 1992

My Family

My family and I live in the suburbs, the North East part of United States. It is Novemember now it is geting cooler, in fact very cold. I have two sisters—Leslie and Lauren; ages 11 and 14. Thay are very nice sisters to. I also have to wonderful parents, named Rob—my dad, and Lisa—my mom. And I also have a very, very cute dog named Tucker, he is one year old, and he is a Sheltie, my favorit kind of dog. And my sister Leslie takes Gymnastics. And my sister Lauren plays soccer. And both of my sisters are proud of themselves. And my mom is a Musician. My dad is a percussionist. I Kelly Bair am just a simple piano player.

Intermittently, cards and gifts continued to arrive for Kelly. "We appreciate everything so much," I told a friend over the phone. "But sometimes it's overwhelming, too."

"Doesn't this show you how absolutely *staggering* it would be if we were to comprehend, all at one time, how much God loves us?" she said.

People fussed constantly over Kelly, sometimes treating her

in baby-like ways. One night when we were at the home of some friends, a woman asked Kelly to sit on her lap and began to raise her voice as if she were talking to a small child. I was aware that Lauren and Leslie were watching, and that jealousy was permeating the air. Invariably, in the car on the way home, the subject surfaced. "Did you see how she was treating Kelly?" Leslie piped up.

Even Kelly agreed. "She was talking to me like I was a baby."

"I know," I said. "People just care a lot, that's all. We can't control how they do it."

"The reason everyone fusses over you and gives you presents all the time is because they think you're going to die," Lauren, said, half disgusted.

The statement hung precariously in the air, an emotional cat finally out of the bag, cautiously stretching itself. No one wanted to be first to acknowledge the thing. But she said it in a way that implied, *Of course you're not going to die, so why all this fuss?*

The car rolled along in the darkness, a container of uncomfortable silence. Eventually we talked it out, clearing the air. For the three sisters, seven years of intimate relationship had effectively sensitized them to one another, and Kelly understood the core of the problem clearly. Unfortunately, she saw it as her problem, possibly her fault:

November 28, 1992
  Hi Jesus., I just wanted to confess my sins, and to tell you how I feel. Right now I feel like I am geting lots of atechen that I don't need. And I feel that Lauren and Leslie shuold get it, to! One night my family was driving home when Mom, Dad, Lauren, and Leslie started talking about gelisey. I do not know who got us into the convrosashon, but I felt realley bad—I was redy to cry because I didean't want to hog up atenchon. Lauren and Leslie need atenchon to!

At dinner a few days later, the subject came up again. And this time it was Kelly's turn to let her feelings out. Her chin started to quiver, and then she set down her fork and began to cry. The chatter dissolved into sympathetic silence.

"What's wrong?" I asked softly.

She choked and sputtered. "I—I'm costing you so much m-m-oney, and—am—causing you so much t-t-trouble." She stopped talking and cried hard. When she could speak again, she looked sympathetically at her sisters. "I'm sorry. I wish you could get more attention, too."

We were all mute for a moment. "Kelly," Rob started, "we have medical insurance to cover the big bills. That paid for your surgery and will cover most of your treatment. We're not really worried about money. We talk about other expenses sometimes, but that's not *your* fault. All of us create expenses in this household."

"And as for causing us trouble," I chimed in, "you're not the trouble. The cancer is the trouble. If we seem upset about it, it's because we feel so bad that you have to go through all this."

"You can't help all this attention; it's not your fault," Leslie said.

"We're not mad at you for getting it. We're just being selfish. I'm sorry," Lauren said.

The issue was not strictly between the girls. We felt it, too. "My life, because of all her hospitalization and care, is so Kelly-consumed," I told a friend. "I can't go to many of Lauren's and Leslie's activities, and I'm often too stressed out to be a good mother to them. They've really been on their own a lot these last few months. I feel like I'm missing out on an important part in their lives, and when this ordeal is over, they'll be all grown up."

I expected to stay in the hospital with Kelly in Philadelphia a day or two prior to Thanksgiving. But after arriving there and going through all the routine tests, her blood counts were not high enough to receive treatment. We drove home, disappointed with the aggravation of having packed and made the long trip for no reason. But the postponement provided us with an unexpected blessing—a holiday weekend at home together, with Kelly on the upside of treatment and feeling fairly well. As it turned out, we had a unique family project to do—one which, I had to admit, excited me more than I thought it would.

Leslie had begged us for two years to get her a trampoline. Each time she mentioned it, we turned her down—too expensive, too dangerous, too much of a slope in the backyard. But out of the blue that weekend came a call from my parents: "If Leslie still wants a trampoline, our neighbors are willing to give theirs away. Their children have outgrown it."

Sometimes, when serendipity's ducks take to following at your heels, it can seem right to do something which previously seemed out of the question. Maybe Leslie had worn us down more than we knew. But with expense out of the picture, Rob suddenly saw a way he could embed the legs of the trampoline underground on one side in order to level it out in the backyard. And danger? Well, something about our lives these days had given the word new meaning. Most of all, however, we needed some fun. To me, the trampoline symbolized something deeper. I didn't know quite what it was, but I was feeling strangely drawn to it.

The day after Thanksgiving, we had the circular apparatus securely installed, leveled into the ground, and supplied with new springs, and a repaired tarp. Our kids and some of the neighborhood children began what would eventually be a regular sight in the backyard—bodies bouncing up and down outside the kitchen window like giddy, out-of-control pistons.

At 11:00 p.m. that same night, I let the dog out. There the trampoline was, looking like a summer swimming pool after all the kids have slid out of it and gone home for the day. The restored surface gleamed sleek and inviting. I turned off the outside spotlight and slipped out through the back door. Dare I? A *mother?*

The moon, high and bright in the sky, beckoned me upward as I stepped onto the buoyant tarp and sprang into the air. The exhilarating movement swept through my being like when I was a kid spending summer days on the high diving board at the pool.

I leapt higher and higher, gulping the fresh, cold air into stale corners of my lungs, relishing the feeling of the wind whipping through my hair. Within minutes I knew it was more than exercise I had been missing these last six months. And it was more than needing to break up and out of the extreme stress. It was *rejoicing* that was absent from my life—that God-given fuel for the heart when caught in the center of life's precarious offerings.

I thought of the Language of Praise class I had taken years before. There I learned that the root meaning for the Hebrew word "rejoice" used in the Old Testament means *to leap up and twirl about.* I remembered the admonition in Philippians and began to quote it rhythmically with each jump: *ReJOICE in the Lord ALways, and aGAIN I say reJOICE.*

Finally, I collapsed onto the tarp. "God," I said, huffing and puffing. "You *knew* Leslie wasn't the only one who needed this!" I stretched my arms and legs out as far as I could and gazed into the beautiful night sky, my heart thumping with exhilaration. "Father, Father, Father! You are so good . . . so very . . . very . . . good."

The following week Kelly's blood counts went up high enough for her to return to Philadelphia for treatment. After settling into our assigned room, we took a walk down the hall to the playroom and happened to see a familiar face. "Christopher! Buddy, how 'ya doin'?" I said, giving him a hug. Kelly and he exchanged smiles. His father, Brian, entered the room and greeted us warmly.

"Tell Kelly how you were on TV, Chris," he said. In his soft voice, Chris described having his wish granted through a Make-A-Wish Foundation and appearing on TV, making a running catch with a Philadelphia Eagles football player.

"Wow!" I said.

"Unfortunately," Brian continued, "the news reporters identified him as terminally ill. Later, people called us and said they couldn't believe he was well enough to run."

There was the label again that jolted the balance of all parents of patients in oncology: *terminally ill.* We were all crusaders for hope, and none of us wanted to hear the term attached to our children or to entertain its definition. Like we had done so often, we quietly let the subject drop and turned our conversation to the task at hand—making our children's journey in the present as upbeat as possible.

17.

Dear Santa,
I would like to get a old fashion sled, lots of thick books, a
puppy, and Jesus Christ!!

Your's truely, Kelly Bair

P.S. Fill my stocking.

"Kelly! Wait 'til you see what we got you!" Leslie announced the minute we came through the door late in the afternoon on December 4th. Exhausted and sick from her second treatment and hospitalization, Kelly made her way to the sofa and flopped down on it. But when she opened the bag Lauren presented to her, her face lit up. So did mine. Out came a soft, red velvet, Santa hat with thick, white fur trim.

"You look adorable! I love it," I said after she put it on. "Thanks, guys. What a perfect gift!"

"It's soft, too," Lauren said. "Not the cheap kind that'll make her head itch."

Two weeks later, Kelly was seated in a wheelchair in front of me in the playroom of Hershey Medical Center, awaiting blood work and her shot of vincristine. The hat dangled winsomely off to one side, the furry ball at the end resting on her shoulder. We were both captivated by a folk singer who had come in to entertain the children with his guitar. I couldn't resist the charm of his silly songs.

"What's your name?" I asked him later. "It means a lot that you would come here. These appointments can get awfully long sometimes. Your songs were great."

"Oh, thanks. My name's Woody Wolfe." He reached into his pocket and pulled out a name card. *Woody Wolfe, Jr.—Christian Musicianary*, I read.

"So you're a Christian."

"Yes, that's why I do this; it's my little mission field, I guess."

"Kelly? We're ready for you to come back," a nurse interrupted from the doorway.

"That's us, Woody . . . Hope to see you again sometime," I said.

Back in one of the treatment rooms, Kelly lay down on the table and dutifully pulled up her shirt. "Count to three," she commanded the nurse. Then she fixed her eyes straight ahead and began to exhale slowly as I had suggested she do to relax and deal with the anxiety of the needle prick.

"Okay, no problem," the nurse cheerfully responded, rubbing her finger over the raised area near Kelly's neck to feel for the placement of the infusaport. She sterilized the area, then counted, "One, two three—good job!" The needle was in—*accessed*, they called it. Kelly let go of my hand. "Now I'm going to draw a little blood . . . you're doing just great."

A vial of blood was obtained and would soon be sent to the lab to check for red and white cell counts, as well as platelets, the clotting agents in the blood. These counts would be monitored carefully throughout each cycle of treatment and could necessitate a transfusion or postpone a hospitalization, depending on their level.

"Okay Kelly, now here's your vincristine," the nurse said, injecting the medicine into the same tube from which she drew the blood. "All right, ready for me to take the needle out? One, two, three—done!"

With that injection, chemotherapy cycle number two was

complete. For the next six cycles, Kelly would receive her chemo at Hershey, permission granted by the doctors at CHOP. Each cycle would begin with an inpatient stay at the hospital, followed by two outpatient appointments. We quickly learned, however, that the treatment schedule was nothing to set our calendar by. If it wasn't blood counts that were low, it might be an overcrowded hospital bed situation which would send us home until a bed became available. All chemotherapy patients, due to their low white cell counts, had suppressed immunity systems, we had been told. This meant taking extra precautions to avoid picking up infections, particularly chicken pox which, if untreated, could be fatal to an oncology patient. It also meant emergency hospitalization in the event of a fever of 101 degrees or more. And so the children with fevers—a condition called *neutropenia*—were rightly given first priority on beds.

"We're done 'til after Christmas, I think!" I told Kelly as we drove out of the hospital parking lot.

"Good," she stated dryly, peeling off her Santa hat once the car was warmed. She laid her head on her pillow and shut her eyes for the duration of the ride.

The next day the clinical care supervisor, Karen, called me. "Kelly's blood counts are borderline and will probably dip lower," she said. "We'd like her to come in for a blood test in a few days to check which direction they're going. It could be she'll need a transfusion. Have you noticed any bruising on her, or unusual fatigue?"

"Fatigue, most definitely. But transfusions this soon?" I asked. "I thought this didn't happen until later in the treatment."

"Every child's different," she said. "Some don't ever need transfusions; others need them all the time."

"My husband has always said that if she needs blood, he really wants to donate for her."

By the next blood check, Kelly was in immediate need of platelets. "I can wait for your husband's red cells, but we can't wait longer for the platelets," Dr. Close told us. "With all the trauma Kelly's brain has suffered from surgery, I don't want to risk any internal bleeding."

So the next day found us in the clinic playroom once again. "Kelly, would you like to join us for some spin art?" said the ever resourceful Lisa, a child-life specialist. I marveled at her wonderful presence with all the children, immediately drawing them in, keeping rowdy ones occupied and under control. Kelly played with the children for a long period of time until her platelets arrived.

"It looks like they're giving me orange juice!" she exclaimed as the nurse attached the tubing to her accessed infusaport. Indeed, the bag of bright orange liquid hanging from the IV pole did look like juice.

"I hate to tell you this, Kelly," the nurse said, "but you'll likely be in here Thursday to get your daddy's red cells." She didn't need to elaborate on what *Thursday* meant. It was Christmas Eve, and no child above the age of five needed to be reminded of it. "The platelets don't take too long, but it takes almost five hours to get the red cells—I'm sorry." She scrunched her face into a pout to sympathize.

"That's okay," Kelly said, laughing. "It doesn't matter."

There was something special about Thursday morning when we arrived at the clinic. Since no routine appointments had been scheduled, it was unusually quiet. The playroom, void of its normal flurry of active children, was tidy and inviting with its red and green paper chain links and shiny star mobiles. The nursing staff, reduced to just a few, were not overly busy and had time to give more personalized attention.

"Your blood's all ready for you," one nurse smiled pleasantly.

Lisa was armed with a supply of suggestions to keep Kelly occupied. "I've got movies, games, and crafts for you, Kelly," she said with a magnetism no child could resist and no parent could help but appreciate.

Three hours into the transfusion, Kelly began to perk up. Her pale cheeks took on a bit of a rosy glow. I marveled at the infusion of life and energy this blood was giving her.

Finally, at two o-clock in the afternoon, we were free to go. Energized, Kelly changed into a bright red sweater, white turtleneck, red and green plaid skirt, white tights, and patent leather shoes. Topped with her Santa hat and now-rosy cheeks, she hopped into the car, and we drove to Grandma and Grandpa's house where the extended family was waiting for us.

Kelly marched right over to Rob and put her arms around his neck. "Daddy, your blood was the best gift anybody ever gave me. Thank you."

18.

Saturday, January 23, 1993

Hi! Its me again, Kelly. today is a pritty day, its suney, clear, and its not a bit cloudy. Right now my dad is geting redy to go reph baskitbal. My mom is doing longrey. Leslie is at gymnastics. Lauren is at county orcastra, she has a consert tomarrow. Right now I feel peaceful and quite fine.

Kelly was halfway through first grade in the winter of 1992, healthy and thriving—or so we thought—when we started attending a different church, not too far from our home. Having come through a painful, six-month detachment from another nearby church, we were anxious to settle down. During our married life, we had changed churches more often than we wanted, due to what we perceived as Holy Spirit-directed shifts regarding my music ministry, or simply out of a desire to find a church that could better blend the unique needs and gifts of Rob's and my contrasting personalities. Our most recent move, however, had been due to neither, but rather to a painful congregational split. We left reluctantly—confused and hurting. Slowly, after several fruitful attempts at reconciliation, we and others were beginning to heal. But it became clear God was not calling us to go back.

"The next place we join," Rob said wearily, after several months of having church at home, "will be our last. I want us to settle in somewhere and die there, and I don't want it to be more than five minutes away." His comments were made flippantly, in great spiritual exhaustion. We had already agreed to put my music ministry gifts on the back burner. First and foremost, our family needed a place to worship God and connect with the body of Christ. If God wanted me to continue with music, it would happen secondarily. If not, we were at peace with my looking for another part-time job.

But no other job opened up. It was a significant bite in our budget to lose my salary from the church we had left the summer before. Finally, while waiting for our dog to get shots at the veterinarian's one morning, I heard the receptionist tell someone on the phone that they were looking for a receptionist/veterinary assistant. My heart quickened. Could this be it? I had wanted to be a veterinarian back when I was 12, and I had secretarial experience from way back. It would be close enough for me to walk to work. In my mind, it was ideal.

"God," I prayed. "I can't see what's ahead in your plan for my life, but if they offer me this job, I will take it. If, for some reason, this isn't at all what you have in mind, let them completely overlook my application."

Why I thought a resumé from a woman with a music degree would catch the attention of a veterinarian is presently beyond me, but they did just what I had asked of God—completely overlooked me.

The Sunday Rob suggested we try a different church—exactly 1.3 miles from our house—I was disillusioned, weak of heart, expectant of nothing from the service, let alone God himself. *Okay, Lord, here we are in a church five minutes down the road. I hope Rob's happy.*

After the opening hymns, the pastor directed us to turn to page #607 in the hymnals. "Let's read together *A Covenant Prayer in the Wesleyan Tradition.*"

"I am no longer my own, but thine," the multi-timbred voices thundered off the walls. The phrase shot straight to my heart and gripped me. It was the exact phrase that months before I had etched into a piece of wood in a park during a painful prayer walk where I had hoped to sort out my confusion over church issues.

"Put me to what thou wilt, rank me with whom thou wilt. Put me to doing, put me to suffering. Let me be employed by thee or laid aside for thee, exalted for thee or brought low by thee . . ." Tears sprang from my eyes. God had thrown out his fishing net, and I was helplessly and wonderfully caught in it. I doubt there was a person there who meant the words more than I did that morning.

The strength of the congregation's voice wrapped me up in its boom and carried me through the rest of it: ". . . Let me be full, let me be empty. Let me have all things, let me have nothing. I freely and heartily yield all things to thy pleasure and disposal. And now, O glorious and blessed God, Father, Son, and Holy Spirit, thou art mine, and I am thine. So be it. And the covenant which I have made on earth, let it be ratified in heaven. Amen."

That moment was the start of a growing attachment to the church. All of us liked it, and, more importantly, we had the sense it was the place we were to be, anointed and chosen by God. Deep within, all five of us believed it.

While our experiences in various congregations had given us a wonderful love for the larger community of faith, as well as a deep appreciation for the many diversified expressions of it, we were concerned about how all these moves were affecting our children. Lauren and Leslie had been baptized as infants in the Lutheran church. But by the time Kelly was born, we were in a Mennonite-affiliated congregation, and so she was dedicated rather than baptized as an infant.

Time and time again, Kelly would raise the question of baptism, concerned somehow that she was the only nonbaptized member in the family. I was intrigued by the urgency in her voice regarding this. One Sunday when she was five, we attended the Lancaster Church of the Brethren where I had grown up. After the service I took her behind the altar area and guided her into the place where I had been baptized when I was 11.

"Daddy, Lauren, and Leslie were sprinkled when they were baptized," I explained. "But in this church, you are baptized under water. It's called baptism by immersion, and you do it when you know you're a believer in Jesus." I took her hand and led her down into the dry tank. "I wore my bathing suit under a long white robe, came down into the nice warm water, and there the pastor helped me go under three times: in the name of the Father, the Son, and the Holy Spirit. Then he prayed for me."

A year later, one week after we began attending Hempfield United Methodist Church, Kelly mentioned it again. "How do they baptize at this church?" she asked out of the blue in the car one afternoon.

"I'm not really sure; I'll have to ask," I answered. "Are you feeling like you want to be baptized? Is that why you bring this up so much?" Kelly was quiet. "Are you worried about something?" I pressed.

"I do want to be baptized—I'm just scared of all those people looking at me."

We had let the issue go for a few months—then, with the onset of her illness, it had moved completely to the back burner. But after her Christmas blood transfusion and the start of another new year, she asked about it again: "Did you find out yet how they baptize people at church?"

I was impressed with her tenacity about this. I studied her face, the color washed out again from another cycle of chemotherapy. Not only was her hair gone, but her once thick, blonde eyelashes and eyebrows were thinned out, too. Her eyes, once sparkly and often mischievous, had lost their sheen. But deep inside them, there was a burning intensity. It was time to address this once and for all. "If you could pick how you want to be baptized, what would you choose?"

Her thin eyebrows furrowed at the question. "I want to be—what's that word?"

"Immersed? Where you go under water?"

"Yes, immersed—I want to be immersed. But would people have to watch me?"

"Well, some should, since it's a public testimony to the church. But with your situation, maybe it could be private. Let me ask Pastor Tom."

By this time, we knew infants were sprinkled in baptism at the church. Perhaps Kelly could be baptized at my home church. But upon further inquiry, I discovered a wonderful fact: our church had an immersion tank behind the altar, just like the one at the church where I was raised, only the tank was hidden under two large floorboards.

"From what I understand," Pastor Tom told me, "the tank was last used 10 years ago."

"Would anyone mind if it were used again?" I asked.

His eyes widened with excitement. "I can certainly ask. This would be absolutely wonderful, although, I've gotta tell ya, I've never done an immersion before."

"I know baptisms are supposed to be public events," I said. "But do you think, because of Kelly's baldness, we could do it privately—perhaps with family and a few significant people with whom she'd feel comfortable without her hat?"

"I don't see why not, under these special circumstances. Let me talk to the property commission about this."

A week later, the pastor reported the good news. "All systems are go! You just pick a date, and we'll try to get it ready."

Our main concern was finding a time at the end of one of Kelly's treatment cycles when she would feel relatively good. Because her hospitalizations were dependent on her blood counts, not the calendar, it was hard to plan. I also had concerns about the chilly weather and her catching cold, since no one knew how well the water heating jets worked in the baptistry. We decided to play it by ear, possibly looking toward a date in March or April, but deciding closer to the time.

The weeks following were marked by multitudinous clinic visits, blood tests, and transfusions. We spent hours upon hours in the waiting room, and while the delightful child-life specialists did everything they could to keep Kelly and all the children occupied, there were times when, for me, boredom crept in heavily. I read books and wrote piles of letters and journals. But it was a wonderful gift to me personally when Rob or grandparents could relieve me from one of the trips.

With all the toxic treatment in her system, Kelly was physically depleted. She required blood transfusions routinely after each cycle now, and often her counts were so slow in coming up that her treatments were postponed for several weeks.

Comparing notes on the phone with my Philadelphia friend, Cindy King, I learned that Christopher had not yet required even one transfusion, and had sped far ahead of Kelly in his treatment cycle.

Kelly's second grade teacher, Mrs. Bear, came to our house every now and then to do tutoring to catch her up from all her absenteeism. Kelly did exceptionally well in school, but many days the teacher and nurse reported that she spent time resting in the health room. Sometimes she felt poorly enough that the nurse called me to come get her—days often coinciding with low blood counts. Mrs. Bear did an excellent job of keeping tabs on Kelly's treatment schedule and progress academically. But the young teacher's swelling midsection would soon bring their work together to a finish.

"Since the baby's due soon," she said to Kelly one afternoon when they were seated together at the dining room table, "we're going to find you a new homebound instructor. You'll really like your new schoolteacher, Mrs. Stephenson. But we're not sure yet whether she'll be able to home-school you."

Kelly continued to eat scantily. That was a source of constant concern to me, especially during the initial weeks of each treatment cycle. Some mornings it was next to impossible to get her to eat or drink anything, let alone take the array of pills I had split into halves or thirds and set before her. Her forehead propped up by her hand, she'd moan and agonize for 10 minutes, it seemed, before I'd quicken the process by announcing that the bus was coming. It was like pulling teeth. *You've got to eat, you've got to drink.* I had become a broken record, and the tune was wearing both of us thin.

Good nutrition was hardly an issue anymore. It was no use fighting and getting both of us upset. Grocery shopping had become an adventure to see what new thing I could buy that might trigger her appetite and stimulate her to eat. The most surefire foods so far were spaghettios and glazed doughnuts. They worked best served not at the table where food was the focal point, but in front of the TV where it could be ingested as an afterthought.

Our least stressful times fell during the week before her next treatment cycle was to begin. That is when she felt the best. Rob called it her "tanking up" phase. Usually we recognized its onset by requests which came in the evening from behind the couch. Kelly lay there to watch TV. "Do we have any glazed doughnuts?" So anxious to get calories into her, I would run to the grocery store late in the evening just to satisfy one of her unusual whims.

The winter was bitter cold at some points, and it wasn't wise for Kelly to play outdoors. We purchased an adorable, thick, winter hat with a great wreath of fur around it and two long, soft ties to cover her ears and go under her neck, but it wasn't sufficient to withstand the cold. Because of her lack of hair and the absence of fat on her bones, Kelly often shivered even indoors. I didn't want to risk her getting overly chilled.

One day, however, when it snowed, she wanted to go out and play so desperately that I finally relented. "Okay, you can go out, but we're going to have to dress you in an awful lot of stuff."

It took nearly 15 minutes to layer her body in enough warmth to weather the elements. When she finally opened the door to go out, overstuffed and nearly lost in the clothing, she was all grins.

Ten minutes later she wanted to come back in. Tired and shivering, she immediately returned to her favorite activities— reading and stringing tiny, colorful beads into necklaces.

2/15/93

Today is a cloudy day. I hate cloudy days! I just finished reading a cople of books. I am very bord right now! I mean really bord! Today I was cleaning the kichon for my mom, I do not like cleaning the kichon! Because you have to tuch other peoples food!

Tuesday, February 16th, we were scheduled to go to Philadelphia for a routine MRI. It had snowed several inches by the time we woke up and more was expected. School was canceled, and I would have postponed our appointment had not Rob, off for the day and looking for a little adventure, decided to try the trip. Lauren and Leslie, weary with the whole hospital and clinic routine, opted to stay home.

Surprisingly, the trip was fairly easy. The staff at CHOP, however, was surprised we made it. "Most of the local people canceled out today," they laughed.

The weather created a little anxiety for me, probably enough to divert my focus away from the reason we had come: to see if the cancer was still in check. But our hopes were high, and neither Rob nor I was overly anxious about the results of this scan.

The nurse practitioner called early the next morning. "Mrs. Bair? I'm calling about Kelly's MRI."

My heart started to beat a little harder.

"I just wanted to let you know that everything's clear. It looks fine. We'll see her again in three months."

19.

In mid-March, Kelly reached the halfway mark in her chemotherapy treatment plan. She completed four cycles which totaled 13 days as an inpatient in the hospital, 28 outpatient visits, and six blood transfusions. No longer was she intimidated by treatment procedures. Hershey Medical Center and its staff began to feel as much like home and family to us as Philadelphia had during radiation treatments.

"Hi Kelly!" Michelle popped her head into the doorway of the outpatient clinic playroom where Kelly was hooked up to yet another bag of platelets. "How ya doin'?" For the sick children, these child-life specialists were as vital as the medications the doctors ordered. Kelly grinned expectantly: *What new activity are we going to do today?*

"Kelly, have you heard about Camp Can-Do? It's a camp just for kids with cancer, and it's absolutely fantastic. You'll be old enough to go this summer. Do you think you might be interested? I get to go and be a counselor for it, and you'll know lots of the kids."

I had my reservations. I couldn't imagine this child, nauseated a large percentage of the time and glued to the family room sofa on a regular basis, enjoying a rustic, "roughin' it" kind of camp experience. She'd never even been away from us overnight except that one night in ICU after surgery. "Would you enjoy something like that?" I asked Kelly.

"I think so," she said cautiously.

"It would help if we knew a little more about it," I told Michelle. "And we'll have to make sure the dates coincide with her treatment schedule so she'll feel well enough to enjoy it."

"Of course," Michelle said. "You can choose either the second or third week in August. Since our hospital staffs the camp medically, the doctors really go out of their way to make sure the treatments don't interfere with the camp weeks. They're quite good about that." She winked at Kelly. "I'll get you an application, and you can think about it, okay? Kids come from all over and it fills up pretty fast, so, if you think you would enjoy it, get your application in soon."

I got out my calendar to check the two camp weeks against my prediction of where Kelly's treatments would fall near that time. "Mommy," Kelly said, watching me, "don't forget to pick a date for my baptism."

I promised I'd talk to the pastor later that afternoon. This did seem to be a good time. Kelly was on the upswing following her last hospitalization, and I figured we could fit in the baptism just before her next treatment.

We took a family hike the following Sunday, a gorgeous first day of spring. We parked our car near Chiques Rock overlooking the Susquehanna River and started hiking a trail still somewhat squishy from the winter thaw.

"The date's all set for your baptism," I told Kelly. "It'll be April 3rd—Palm Sunday—at two o'clock in the afternoon. And since it'll be private, you need to think about whom to invite to it."

That settled, Kelly went ahead of us on the trail, stopping to pick up stones and other interesting objects she found. "Are you sure you feel like hiking this whole trail?" I called.

"She's fine," Rob said, squeezing my shoulder. "She loves this. Don't worry about her. Remember the hill at Safe Harbor last fall? *You* stayed at the bottom, and *she* made it to the top!"

"You're right," I sighed. "I just can't seem to get out of this protective mode."

"Well, relax and have a good time. This is good for her—and you."

He was right. Within an hour I was refreshingly winded, and Kelly seemed to have unusual reserves of strength to spare. For the first time I began to see what had been obvious to Rob all along. We had a real nature lover on our hands. Her passion for the outdoors—something he shared with her a lot more than I realized, on fishing trips and miscellaneous fresh air outings—fueled her spirit in a way that food couldn't touch and toxic medicine couldn't completely squelch.

Rob, Lauren, and I belonged to a music worship team which did concerts in churches once or twice a month. Right before she became ill, Kelly expressed interest in being a part of the interpretive movement group which included other adults and children. As the new fall season began, Bonnie, the leader of the dance group, was anxious to include Kelly as much as she felt she could participate.

The night of her first performance, I pulled out the wig we had bought. Kelly had worn it only once before. "You probably should wear this so that you don't distract people away from the whole effect with your hat." I adjusted it on her head. Months before it had matched her hair nicely. Now it hung limply around her thinner, color-depleted face. "What do you think?" I asked her, both of us facing the mirror as I fixed loose strands of hair while she perched on the vanity in the bathroom.

"It's okay, I guess."

"All right then, let's try it tonight and see how it works."

After the program Kelly walked with me to my car while Rob loaded his drums and Lauren's cello in the other. "Mommy, I was so proud of myself tonight," she said.

"You felt you did a good job?" I asked, unlocking the car door. I paused to look at her face in the dim light of the street lamps.

"I did okay, but—" she paused, looking upward, "—mostly I just really felt open to God, and that makes me feel proud."

I looked at her in disbelief. I knew Bonnie worked hard to sensitize the group to the Holy Spirit as they gave the concerts. Obviously she had succeeded, even with the youngest.

"That's really wonderful, Kelly. That's what this is all about."

Several months later at another one of our concerts, I lingered afterwards, talking with several friends I hadn't seen in a while. Kelly came up repeatedly to ask me if we could please get going, but each time I put her off. Finally, she came up out of sheer exasperation and interrupted the conversation: "If you don't please come now, I'm gonna pull off this itchy wig right here in front of everybody!"

I did end my conversation, but not because she threatened me. Reprimanding her for her rudeness, I was reminded again of how necessary it was to keep ongoing discipline happening in our parenting. It helped to take the edge off the cloyingly sweet attention lavished upon her, and to make her feel "normal."

We yearned for normalcy, questioned what it really meant for anyone, tried hard to fabricate it, and often lived with the fantasy that some day we might actually return to what we once thought it was. The word would surface occasionally in conversation, but, like an elusive butterfly, we had already begun to learn that "normal" cannot be pinned down—only enjoyed in the moment before it changes direction and moves on.

20.

◦⌇◦

I would like to invite you to my baptism at my church. This is a very special time for me, and it would mean a lot to me if you could come!

† Love in christ!
   Kelly

April 4 - Palm Sunday
2:00 P.M.
Hempfield United Methodist Church

You are invited to
our home afterward for light
refreshments and fellowship.

(This baptism is being held privately out of
respect for Kelly's appearance self-consciousness.
We welcome you, the body of Christ, who have supported
her spiritually as well as affirmed her physically!
Thank you for your abiding love!)

The weather itself seemed to shout "Hosanna!" that crisp, glorious Palm Sunday morning, the day commemorating Christ's celebrated entry into Jerusalem. When Jesus approached the great city, his heart broke as he looked upon it. Weeping loudly, he cried, "If you had only known on this day what would bring you peace—but now it is hidden from your eyes . . . for you did not recognize the time of God's coming to you."

Given only mustard seed morsels and a few simple tools, children are vigorous and productive gardeners of their faith. Intuitively, before the weeds of the wayward world can choke the tender plants, they nurture their faith as tall as the sky and learn to see truth through the brilliant kaleidoscope of their unhindered hearts. "Of such," Jesus said, "is the kingdom of heaven."

Rob and I stood humbly before Kelly's garden—as we had before Lauren's and Leslie's—watching her cultivate the soil of her faith with zeal. "The time changes tomorrow," I had told her the night before. "We have to get up an hour earlier."

"Good!" she replied happily. "I'll get to be baptized sooner."

The trustees of the church went to loving lengths to prepare the baptistry for this event. The men gave the walls a coat of fresh paint and meticulously scrubbed the tank. After the morning services were over, we could hear them filling it with water.

At home after lunch, Kelly changed out of her church clothes and eagerly slipped into her brand new tea-length dress, covered with a print of pastel spring flowers. I smoothed the peach-colored satin ribbon around her waist and tied it behind her. She slipped into her tights and buckled her new white shoes. "Pastor Tom said that long ago they used to give people a whole new outfit to wear when they were baptized," I told her, "to symbolize their new life in Christ."

Standing in the doorway of her bedroom, I watched her check herself in the mirror and place her new, white, floppy hat on her head, carefully turning it so the flower was fashionably off-center. "You look absolutely lovely," I said, fastening a necklace with a tiny gold cross around her neck. "What a special day, huh?"

At church we greeted family and friends as they gathered, then tested the water in the voluminous baptismal tank. It was cold, not having heated as we had hoped, even though they kept pouring extra pots of hot water into it. "Just bear it the best you can," I told her. "I'll be waiting with lots of towels as soon as you come out."

The small congregation gathered on one side of the sanctuary. After we sang a hymn, Pastor Tom called Kelly forward and gestured to her to stand beside him. "Brothers and sisters in Christ," he began, "through the sacrament of baptism we are initiated into Christ's holy church. We are incorporated into God's mighty act of salvation and given new birth through water and the Spirit. All of this is God's gift, offered to us without price."

Turning to her, he spoke tenderly. "Kelly, on behalf of the whole church, I ask you: Do you renounce the spiritual forces of wickedness, reject the evil powers of this world, and repent of your sin?" These were big concepts for a seven-year-old, pulled like heavy volumes from the attic of the centuries. But like a child exploring and discovering them on a dreary, rainy afternoon, she had eagerly uncovered them and asked us to interpret her find.

"Remember when you were four and you did that dance where you were fighting the devil?" I had asked her the day before when Pastor Tom reviewed the service with us. "Well, that's what it means to renounce the spiritual forces of wickedness and reject the evil powers of this world. It means you'll live your life hating all the things that hurt people and that make them turn away from God. And when you repent of your sin, it means you turn away from trying to do anything without God. You live your life with Jesus at the center of all your thinking."

She had nodded with understanding, and now, in front of a host of witnesses, she paused, her face intent, pondering the words Pastor Tom asked her. She was not interested in rushing the ritual, or, it seemed, overly conscious of the 50 or so people gathered to witness this event. "I do," she spoke firmly.

"Do you confess Jesus Christ as your Savior, put your whole

trust in his grace, and promise to serve him as your Lord, in union with the church which Christ has opened to people of all ages, nations, and races?"

"I do."

We sang several hymns, and then I took her back to the corridor behind the organ to prepare for the baptism. As I helped her change into her bathing suit, we could hear the strains of the people continuing to sing in the sanctuary: *Children of the heavenly Father safely in his bosom gather; nestling bird nor star in heaven such a refuge e'er was given* . . .

I slipped a white, terry cloth tunic over her. *Neither life nor death shall ever from the Lord his children sever; unto them his grace he showeth, and their sorrows all he knoweth* . . .

From my station behind the wall, I watched Pastor Tom, wearing a long white robe, enter the water and invite the people up to the altar area so they could see. I couldn't see them from where I stood, but I could hear the rustle of suits and dresses as people settled themselves into comfortable positions just above the water's edge. All eyes, I imagined, like mine, held Kelly in their gaze as she, looking small and vulnerable, took his outstretched hand and stepped into the water. Her shoulders tensed from the cold.

"Kelly," he said, placing one hand at the back of her neck and the other over her nose, "I baptize you in the name of the Father . . . " He gently pushed her head down into the water, after which she came up with a gasp and shuddered from the shock of the cold water. "The Son . . . " She went under again and reacted the same way. "And the Holy Spirit."

After the third time, she stood shivering while he laid his hands on her head and prayed: "The Holy Spirit work within you, that, being born through water and the Spirit, you may be a faithful disciple of Jesus Christ."

Tears silently baptized the cheeks of some of those in attendance—grandparents, aunts, uncles, cousins, both pastors and their wives, and two of Kelly's Sunday School teachers, along with a few long-time family friends.

Having received the blessing, Kelly opened her eyes and turned to climb out of the water. I received her trembling body into huge towels and held her to myself for warmth. "You did it, Kelly. You are finally, after all this time of waiting, *baptized.*" I kissed her cheek and patted her head dry.

She smiled, teeth chattering. "Mommy, it was sooo cold!" We had decided it would be easier to stay and greet people at the church instead of back at our house. When she was dressed again and came out to greet the people, she was still trembling. In the Fellowship Hall where everyone gathered for refreshments, Rob took off his jacket and put it on her. Covering almost the entire length of her dress, it extended her arms into handless flaps as she gave and received hugs. Settling into a chair to open a few small gifts and eat a piece of cake, she finally stopped shivering.

That evening as we tucked her into bed, she spoke contentedly of the day, of this new step in her spiritual pilgrimage. We prayed with her, constructing a protective fence of blessing around her burgeoning garden of faith, then kissed her goodnight, securing the gate behind us.

But even parents are limited in their ability to protect these precious terrariums and their tender gardeners who are like young, vulnerable game under the watchful eye of cunning predators. They, too, are ripe for attack by the devil who, the disciple Peter said, "prowls around like a roaring lion looking for someone to devour."

Just after dawn I awoke to the sound of Kelly calling my name. "M-m-mommy," she said standing beside my bed, her thin body trembling under her nightgown. "I had a really bad dream."

Instinctively I rolled onto my side and opened the covers like a clamshell. She quickly crawled in beside me, and I closed them over her, pulling her against me for warmth. "What was it about?" I asked sleepily, kissing her head.

"A man with long, sharp claws was scraping them all over my skin and making me bleed," she whimpered. "Is this what happens after you get baptized?"

My mind angrily recoiled against this horrific picture as I groped for a response. I prayed quietly, desperately. *God, does this child get no rest from everything that's trying to assault her? What's going on here?*

Into my confusion dropped a thought. I went with it. "All I can think of is that right after Jesus was baptized he went out into the wilderness where the devil tried to tempt him into not trusting in God. I don't think the devil likes it when children love and want to follow God." I stroked her arm gently. "But you don't have to worry. Jesus spoke God's truth to the devil, and the devil finally left him. Jesus can help you do that, too."

I didn't mince words with her anymore regarding spiritual warfare. This child was far beyond the rosy enclosure I would have chosen for her. In fact, she seemed innocently immersed in a physical and spiritual battle, and so I relied upon the only weapons I knew could touch it—scripture and prayer. I clung to the scriptural admonition: *Resist the devil, and he will flee.* I prayed softly for her, her head with its precious new growth of hair tucked under my chin. Rob, turning on his side and nestling close to us, reached over me and stroked her arm. Soothed, we all soon fell back to sleep.

Every night following that nightmare, Kelly begged for prayer before bed, particularly for her dreams. Rob and I spent long periods of time comforting her and praying, assuring her of Christ's love and care, reminding her to call upon the name of Jesus when she felt scared. Many nights she'd crawl into bed with Lauren, who had the only double bed among the three of them. But Leslie often slept with Lauren—the bed and closeness having become a family refuge for both of them during a year of parental absence, both physically and emotionally. And so some nights—her sister's bed already occupied—Kelly was forced to return to her own.

Four weeks later, after the completion of chemotherapy cycle number five, I awoke to the sound of Kelly calling to us from her bed. I moved quickly out of bed and to her room. "What's the matter?"

"I don't feel good—and I'm really cold."

I got the thermometer, sterilized it, and slipped it under her tongue. It registered 102 degrees. "Looks like we go to the hospital—now."

I woke Rob. "Kelly's got a fever. Could you please call the hospital and tell them we're coming while I get dressed." I glanced at the clock; it was 1:30 a.m.

"Do you want me to drive you?" he asked.

"No, there's no point in you losing a night's sleep before work tomorrow. We'll be okay; I can sleep at the hospital."

The hospital unfortunately had to move another child into a semi-private room in order to give Kelly a private room when we arrived. Hershey had a policy of doing this for oncology patients, due to their suppressed immunity systems. Kelly was immediately accessed and hooked up to IV medicines. Within the day, her blood counts required transfusions for platelets and packed red cells. The following day, as well, she needed even more platelets. Three days following that, she needed yet another transfusion of platelets. I stayed with her the first two nights, and Rob stayed with her on the weekend. Her temperature had returned to normal within a couple of days, but because her white cell blood count was so poor, we couldn't go home.

"How long do you think we'll be in here?" I asked a nurse.

"Oh, it's not uncommon to stay for 10 or 12 days for something like this," she said, checking the long tubing that extended from the IV machine.

Ten or 12 days! It was only day five. Kelly groaned when I looked at her. "Looks like it's lemonade time," I said, trying to sound cheerful.

"When life gives you lemons," she finished for me, rolling her eyes in disgust.

Because the child-life specialists were so industrious, the following days were peppered with activities, and they became more bearable. They threw a cookie-decorating party in the playroom, sent invitations to join them for pizza in the hall or doughnuts in the lounge, and provided videos, books, and games. But by day seven, Kelly's spirits had plummeted. "I can't even go to my school festival," she moaned.

"What's the matter?" Lisa said, poking her face into the room. "Why so down?"

"She's disappointed to have to miss her school festival tomorrow. She's missed a lot of things this year—you know, picture day, school concerts, field trips, stuff like that."

Lisa stuck her lower lip out. "Aw, Kelly, we'll just have to see what we can do about that, won't we?" She wore a mischievous smile as she turned to leave. "I have to go home for supper. I'll see you tomorrow, and maybe, just maybe—there'll be a surprise. I can't tell you any more. See ya, kiddo."

The next day Lisa had risen to the occasion. She engineered a festival in the playroom, complete with penny candies, bubble gum, games, and stuffed animals for prizes. "Our sour lemons squeezed into some pretty sweet lemonade, don't you think?" I asked Kelly later in the day. She grinned, her lips tightly pressed together and bulging slightly over a huge wad of fresh bubble gum.

Towards the end of her stay, the nurses permitted Kelly to go outside with her IV pole onto the huge lawn in front of the medical center. There, with the rest of the family who came to visit, we breathed in the fresh air and watched Tucker—on his first hospital visit ever—frolic in the grass. After returning home a few days later, Kelly wrote this in her journal:

May 18, 1993

Hi, I'm back! I haven't writen in a long time! It has been almost a year! Yesterday I found out that one of the kids in my school class broke out with chicken pox! I just got back yesterday from the hospital. I went to the hospital becase I got a fever. I had to stay in the hospital for 12 whole days! I feel much better now!! It is almost a year from when I had my brain surgery! They got all the tumer out of me, yay! I'm almost at the end of my chemo! Only 3 more sycles of chemotherapy left! After I am all doen, my whole family will have a big party! I will not be able to go to school because someone has chicken pox! I have a homebound teacher now, so she can teach me at home. Her name is Mrs. Kuster. Write to you soon!

One week later we traveled to Philadelphia for another routine MRI. In the waiting room we met a young fellow from Texas who had a brain tumor removed six years before. "He's doing just great," his mother said.

He made it past the five-year mark, I marveled. It was every oncology parent's greatest hope, and the medical testimony of this boy encouraged me. When Kelly's scan was again clear, we began to anticipate the end of chemotherapy in the fall. I found myself concerned less and less with survival issues, and more with what it would mean to live with a long-term survivor.

Side effects from the radiation may manifest themselves one to five years after radiation is completed, I recalled reading in our literature and hearing the radiation oncologist reiterate. I thought back to a boy in a wheelchair we met at the Ronald McDonald House—a brain tumor survivor of four years who, due to the damage from radiation, couldn't keep food down. His mother had cornered me in the kitchen one day, out of the hearing of each of our children. "I can't believe your daughter is *walking* and seems to be doing so well." She went on to describe her son's plight, and, after she finished, I went back to my room and cried, partially out of tremendous sympathy for them, but also because I realized it could have been our story, too.

While all the oncology personnel cheerfully reminded the newly bald children that their hair would grow back and might even come in curly or a different color, one doctor told me that Kelly's hair would probably never return at the heavily radiated tumor site.

Now, armed with success stories of survivors and articles on the increasing survival rates of children with cancer, I began to think about her quality of life. What about her ability to learn? What about her social life? Would a guy want to date a girl with no hair on the lower back half of her head? Would a young man want to marry a young woman with a medical history like hers?

21.

The teacher stood inside the door of her classroom, receiving the line of thirsty, winded second graders who filed in after recess. "Mrs. Stephenson," said one little boy, "Kelly took her hat off for a little while at recess today."

It was late May, the weather was unseasonably warm, and the doctor had given approval for Kelly to return to school. "She was probably hot with it on," the teacher said. A few classmates hovered close by to confer about this noteworthy event. "You know," she continued, "at home with her family, Kelly hardly ever wears her hat. Wouldn't it be wonderful if she could feel that comfortable around us, too, so that if she wanted to take it off, she could?"

The hat became a symbol of sorts for the little girl with the serious illness—her identifying feature in an elementary school of over 700 students. It was an easy point of reference for a student who didn't know her name: "You know who I mean—that little girl with the hat."

Kelly lost her hair just when the floppy "Blossom" hats, named after the television star of the same name, started to appear in stores and become popular. For us, they were more than a comfortable and stylish alternative to wigs, bandannas, or baseball caps, which she couldn't wear because of her scar.

They were emblems of hope, coverings of blessing on that part of Kelly which had become the focal point of our lives—her precious head.

On that spot, where everything that was Kelly seemed to be centrally located, disease had assaulted, surgery had scathed, and treatment toxins had made their strongest statement. But here also was the place of our most poignant connections— through eyes that held great wells of thought, eyebrows that spelled contentment, fear, or disgust, and lips which formed the words of her heart.

While we loved all of her physical being, it was her head, her *defenseless* head, which commanded the attention of our spirits and directed the course of our prayers. And so we bought hats to bless her, warm her, protect her from the curiosity of strangers—piling fun and a touch of beauty upon her.

Lauren dubbed them, "The Kelly Collection," and they seemed to multiply in number every time we went shopping. I could trace the course of her entire ordeal by the hats she wore—hot pink safari for the summer in Philadelphia, white with blue and white checks and a daisy for the end of treatment and the beginning of school, black velveteen with red and blue plaid for fall, Santa-style for Christmas, blue denim to alternate with the black velveteen in the winter months, the fur-lined one with ties for outdoors, and—finally—the lightweight, dressy white one with the flower that she inaugurated at her baptism, and which became her all-time summer favorite.

School had come to an end, and the neighborhood children were coming regularly to jump on our backyard trampoline. Kelly jumped, too, with her neighborhood friends. The ringing doorbell was Tucker's cue. He would race out the front door and around to the backyard to join in the action, barking urgently for the kids to throw balls for him to fetch.

We were well into our family's summer groove: Rob would leave by 6:50 a.m. to work at his summer job on the maintenance crew in the school district, and the kids, fallen into lazy new sleeping patterns, would get up late morning. Rising when Rob left, I routinely enjoyed at least two hours of solitude before Lauren, the lark of the bunch, would get up. Kelly always rose last, mornings never having been her prime time. Now, with all her sickness in the last year, they had become the worst and least favorite part of her day.

On a morning late in June, after Rob kissed me good-bye, I settled down at the kitchen table in front of the windows with the newspaper and a cup of tea. A cool morning breeze redolent of honeysuckle rustled the corners of my paper. Bird songs filled in the background. I looked forward to an hour or more of meditation and prayer.

I had barely finished my drink when I heard the top step on the staircase creak, followed by soft footsteps padding downward. Lauren up so soon? I turned around to see who would emerge from the landing.

Kelly did. "Well, this is unusual—good morning," I said, turning back to my paper and expecting her to say nothing more. I thought she would switch on her favorite TV shows and flop down on the sofa to watch them.

Instead, she came up behind me and put her hand on my arm. "Mommy," she pleaded, her voice tender but full of something—like bubbling water underneath a capped fountain.

I finished the paragraph I was reading, then looked up into her face. She looked different—soft and melted, exuding something undefinably sweet—like every bitter morsel of suffering she had ever known had been dissolved in its wake. "What's the matter?"

"Mommy, I had the *best dream!*" she said, her eyes wide and filled with light. "I dreamed I was with Jesus."

"How did you know it was Jesus?"

"I just *knew,*" she responded. "We were eating together."

"Where?"

She paused wistfully, then said with great tenderness, "At a table for two."

I felt transformed by her words and the soft look on her face.

A table for two? Had she ever even heard that term before? "What were you eating?"

"I don't remember any food being there, but I *know* we were eating. Oh Mommy, I feel *so close* to God!"

With those words, she turned to go get herself a cereal bowl, another rarity at this early hour of the morning. I followed her face with my eyes, memorizing its glow, marveling at its countenance. Deeply stirred by her description of this intimate encounter, I pondered her words deeply. I looked upon the dream as a wonderful gift of comfort—a magnificent, victorious cancellation of the nightmare she'd had the morning after her baptism. I received it as a harbinger of hope, culminating a year of tremendous warfare in the physical and spiritual realms for her. I held the dream in my heart and let its sweetness roll over my tongue again and again whenever I told it to others.

July 10, 1993

It's Sunday morning and I'm ready to live this day! I'm not going to church today because I don't feel good. I woke up at 6:30 this morning and then I went back to sleep, and then I woke up again and took a shower. I didn't see that the curtain was outside of the tub, so all this water came out of the tub and onto the floor. Right now I'm going to play with my marbles. Mabey I'll wright some more later. Bye.

Kelly finished her sixth cycle of chemotherapy in June. But her blood counts didn't rise sufficiently so that she could receive her July treatment and then recover from it before going to Camp Can-Do. She had registered for the week of August 15-21. "Let's wait to give Kelly her next treatment until after she gets back from camp," Dr. Close said in the examination room. "It's possible CHOP will even let us knock off the last cycle all together. They normally don't like children to exceed a year with their treatment."

This news was wonderful. "Can I get my hopes up?" I asked.

"Better not, just in case, but I'll check and let you know." She looked into Kelly's face. "You have a wonderful time at camp, okay?"

Kelly smiled. By now she had heard so many camp stories that she was looking forward to it with unparalleled excitement. "Mommy," she said one day when I was probing a little too deeply about whether she'd really enjoy an entire week away from home. "You don't understand. I need to go—*to be with my own kind.*"

The differentiation had finally happened, and, while it startled me briefly, I knew she was right. Hard as we tried to empathize with her and faithfully as we had walked beside her, we truly didn't know what it was like for her to be bald in a world of heads with shining hair, to be seriously ill in a world of people complaining about sore throats.

July 12, 1993

Hi! I just got back from Lisa's house. I had a good time! I finished the next book in the seiries of Bunnicula! And I can't wait to read the next book! I don't have much to say, so, bye.

July 14, 1993

Hi, yesterday I went with my Ma-Ma and Pop-Pop to Borders Bookstore and got the last two books for the Bunnicula sereis! I just started the next book this morning. It's good. Lauren is at Keswick. It's a camp for cristion youth. Yesterday Leslie got her braces off! She said her teeth felt slimey and big. She is so glad they took them off! I'm very bord now! I have nothing to do! I'll serch around my room and find something. Bye.

It was the next to last week in July, and we had just returned from a three-day jaunt to Inner Harbor in Baltimore. We needed to remain within accessible distance of a hospital, and this was the farthest point we felt we could go. It had refueled us tremendously as a family, and we took a lot of pictures, but not quite enough to finish the roll of film.

Late afternoon that day, Kelly came downstairs in her baptismal dress. "What are you wearing *that* for?" I asked. She looked particularly healthy and pretty. Then I noticed she was wearing makeup.

"Lauren's taking pictures of me," she announced happily, and took off out the back door. Outfit number two passed by me shortly thereafter—this time striped biker shorts, matching top, pink safari hat, and sunglasses. Later, it was a light blue denim jumper with white T-shirt and white hat. By now my curiosity was sufficiently aroused. I went outside to find Kelly posed in the front yard, lying on the grass on her stomach, tenderly touching the petals of some purple pansies.

"Move a little to the left so the light's better," Lauren instructed. Kelly contentedly obliged. She was obviously enjoying herself.

We got the film developed within a few days. After flipping through our treasured but uninspiring vacation photos, I found my mouth falling open when I came to one of Kelly in her baptismal dress, sitting on the front stoop, her face turned upward and scrunched with delight. Another of her in her jumper had Tucker beautifully poised under a tiny biscuit in her hand. Lauren had placed a bright, deep pink hibiscus between them for color contrast. There were eight pictures, all striking, beautifully centered and artistic.

"Lauren," I called from where I was sitting. "These shots you took of Kelly are *excellent*. I can't believe they were done by a 15-year-old with a $49 camera." Lauren's artistic eye was not new to me. Her drawings had often inspired me. But underneath my surface admiration was a response so deep I groped for clarity. Was the beauty of these pictures due to the loving relationship the two of them enjoyed and the fun they had doing this project?

Kelly had always been near to the center of her older sister's adoring heart. I will never forget when nine-year-old Lauren returned from a five-day trip with her grandparents. She set her things down inside the door, and her eyes locked like radar onto her 22-month-old sister. She rushed to her, fell to her knees, and embraced her. Watching from behind Kelly, I saw tears squeeze out from Lauren's closed eyelids as she pressed Kelly's tousled, blonde head to her cheek and held her for what seemed like an eternal moment.

These pictures had certainly been taken through that same adoring eye. But there was something else I was recognizing—something beyond artistic talent. Could Lauren have been *anointed* when she took these? *Why?* my heart wondered. Why did I feel I had something in my hands that was of inordinate value?

For reasons I could not explain, I removed the negatives from the envelope and tucked them in the dining room hutch for safekeeping. I would need them, I knew. But I did not know why.

22.

It was 4:00 a.m., July 27. Kelly's voice penetrated my sleep. I slipped out of bed and went to her bedside. "I have a headache," she moaned.

"Is it bad?"

"No, but it's bothering me." I went downstairs for Tylenol, gave her some, and she went back to sleep.

At 7:30 I tapped her gently. "Kelly, you have to get up. Lauren and Leslie have orthodontist appointments this morning, and, I'm sorry, but you have to go along."

She groaned in protest. "I don't feel good."

"Is your headache gone?"

"Yes, but I still don't feel good." I thought little of it, since early morning misery had become part of the routine throughout the entire year.

"I'll carry you out to the car, and you can sleep with your pillow in the back," I said, slipping some shorts and a pair of sandals on her. "You can stay in your T-shirt." I scooped her up and carried her down to the car, something I did routinely when we had to go somewhere and she didn't feel well.

At the orthodontist's I parked under a tree, rolled down the windows of the van while the other two went in for their appointments, and pulled a book from my purse while Kelly slept.

Fifteen minutes later, she awoke. From her entertainment stash under the seat she pulled a book. "Mommy, can I read *James and the Giant Peach* to you?"

I looked at her, amazed at her energy for reading aloud, especially on a muggy morning when she didn't feel well. "Sure," I said. "I'll come back there and sit next to you."

She sat up and opened her book, wetting her lips with her tongue and swallowing carefully before taking a good breath. "It— it—"

She sighed, disgusted. "It—"

I helped her begin, reading the first phrase for her, but I was baffled by her hesitation. Kelly was a superb reader. I chalked it off to grogginess.

She began again. "It— it—"

She stopped all together and shut the book, frustrated. "I know the words—I just can't tell you what they are."

Fear rose up within me and shot through my heart. It was exactly one year since the start of radiation treatment, the time we were told when long-term side effects could begin to manifest themselves. The words of a mother at a Philadelphia brain tumor workshop we had attended nine months before came crashing back into my awareness: *My daughter used to be an excellent reader, but she's now in a brain-injured classroom because of the radiation.*

My mind reeled from my worst imagining and groped for bearings in the turbulent sea tossing it. "Kelly, let's try it again—take your time." I tried to sound relaxed, nonchalant.

She reopened the book and tried again, unsuccessfully. Wrinkling her face in frustration, she sank down into her pillow and closed her eyes. "It's no use—I can't do it."

My eyes stung from the angry tears that welled up in them. It had happened . . . my fears had been realized. "Why don't you rest some more," I said, getting up and patting her legs reassuringly as she stretched them out over the rest of the seat. I climbed into the front of the van and opened my book to appear like I was reading.

In my mind's eye a gaping abyss yawned open before me, and the voice of a castigating spirit rose up out of it. *Fool! Did you really think God would protect her from that devastating radiation? Ha!—all that wishful thinking about God's protective wing!* My chest tightened with emotion and my forehead dampened with perspiration. I kept my face aimed toward the driver's wheel and weathered the clamor of this spiritual battle in silence.

Radiation is powerful stuff, the dismal voice reasoned more calmly. *And God doesn't go against natural laws.*

The abyss seemed to close up, leaving a vast, desolate plain in its wake. The horror I felt now turned to hurt. *God, was your wing not enough? You promised to protect her from the radiation, to cover her defenseless head. I felt so certain this was your word to me! Have you now taken away reading, her greatest joy? Will you strip this child of everything she loves?*

The thought of Kelly having learning problems was wrenching enough, but even more devastating was feeling betrayed by my truest Friend—abandoned, made to look foolish for having misinterpreted his spirit. *Did I not hear you right? What about the night a year ago when you promised—or so I thought—to protect her from radiation harm, when it seemed all heaven opened up to comfort and assure me of your power and your presence. Was I making this up?*

I thought of the framed picture my sister had given me the year before, after I told her about the assurance God gave me in prayer through the line in the hymn, *Jesus, Lover of My Soul.* The picture was of a mother eagle spreading her strong, expansive wing over her tiny, fuzzy, baby eaglet. "Look," Abby had said. "It couldn't be more appropriate. They're *bald* eagles." The picture had been yet another confirmation of the promise of God's care. Now I was riddled with doubt.

My heart pounded heavily in my chest. I turned to look at Kelly for fear my internal clamor would awaken her. Her eyes were still shut. I wiped my eyes on the sleeve of my shirt and ached mournfully. *Your sheep are supposed to know your voice. Am I, or am I not, one of yours?*

The questions seemed to mingle and hang heavy with the humidity outside. A bumblebee bobbed lazily around my side-view mirror, then rose up and over the car.

When the girls returned from their appointments a little later, they wakened Kelly and chattered excitedly about going swimming that afternoon. I welcomed the conversation as it diverted their attention from me and kept them from probing into my pain.

That evening in private, when Rob returned from work, I told him what had happened and poured out my fears to him. After supper, he asked Kelly if she wanted to read to him outside on the trampoline. She happily responded, undaunted by her earlier difficulties, back to being thrilled to have a listening audience.

Through the kitchen window I watched the two of them snuggle against a sofa pillow in the center of the circular tarp. Kelly settled against Rob, propping her head on his arm. They opened the book and raised it slightly to let the setting sun illuminate the pages. With the open book covering her face, I couldn't see whether she was reading or not. But after five minutes I relaxed a little—the book had not closed.

"She read fine," he told me when they came in an hour later as dusk began to fall. "Whatever was wrong this morning is gone now." We exchanged looks of guarded relief.

"What's going on?" I asked him, frustrated. "Is the devil trying to get me to doubt God's word, or is this the slow, irregular onset of a long-term problem? I feel like I'm being toyed with."

Saturday, July 31, 1993
    Yesterday was my birthday. Today it is kind of cloudy outside and hot. Other than that it has been a beautiful morning. This morning Lauren and I made necklesess with my new beads! It was fun to be with Lauren at that time. Well, I got to go. Bye.

Sunday, August 1, 1993

Hi, today is a wonderful day to be alive! It's nice and sunny outside. And I might go swimming! I feel so good today. I feel like I have been renewed by the Lord! Today in church we had communion. That was fun. Today my dad is going to put my new corckbord that I got for my birthday on my wall. Well, I have no more to say, so, bye.

Monday, August 2, 1993

Hello, I just woke up and took a shower. Now I feel really awake! My mom and my sister and my dad might go to a musicle place to buy a chella for Lauren. And when they are goen I might get to go swimming.

Tuesday, August 3, 1993

Hi, today I woke up and was about to get up when Lauren held me back from geting out of her bed. She said, "Kelly, don't get up. I don't like you getting a shower before me, so stay in bed." It made me kind of mad. She doesn't always have to be the first one to get in the shower!

Wednesday, August 4, 1993

Hi! Today Leslie went to gymnastics and when she came back, she didn't feel good. But now she is better. Outside it is sunny and nice. Lauren is playing Nintendo, and Dad is at work. Dad works maitnins in the summer. On the fifteeth of Agaust I am going to Camp Can-Do. It's a camp for cancer kids. See ya, bye.

Thursday, Agaust 5, 1993

Hi. I told Leslie a seacrete, and she told my dad. It was about school. Sometimes I get myself worked up to make me not feel good. That happend in school. I was mad that Leslie told Dad that that happend. But now I understand that was a seacrete she should be abele to tell Dad because it was kind of a problem. Now I am fine. Bye.

A TABLE FOR TWO

Friday, Agaust 6, 1993

Hello. Today it's very rainy! I went to see Snow White with Ma-Ma and Pop-Pop today. That was kind of fun. Now I'm bord and tired and just sick of life! I'm just depresed. Bye.

Saturday, Agaust 7, 1993

Today it is pretty sunny and dry. My mom and my dad are teaching Sunday school tomarow. They haven't doen that in a while. Leslie is babysiting. Lauren is in her room doing I don't know what. Dad is downstairs doing dishes. Mom just came home from the church and is talking to Dad. Got to run. Bye.

Sunday, Agaust 8, 1993

Hi, it's the evening now and I almost forgot to write. Today we went to church and stayed there for a picnic! It was fun! I drew a really good pictshure of my dad today. Mom said it was my best drawing. I am really, really, really proud of myself! I have to go to bed. Bye.

Monday, Agaust 9, 1993

Hi! Linda is coming over this afternoon to stay for a week. She is sleeping in my room. I will sleep with Lauren. Today it is sunny and hot. There's a little wind but I don't mind, it feels good! Next Sunday I go to camp! I can't wait! It is going to be so much fun! Got to run. Bye.

Tuesday, Agaust 10, 1993

Hi! Today is warm outside. You can hear all the birds singing! They are beutiful! God has blesed this day with song and beuty! Today is Mom's and Dad's aniversery. I'm going to make a card for them! I did not eat brekfast yet, and I think I should, so bye.

Wednsday, Agaust 11, 1993

Hi! Tonight there is going to be a meateor shower! Our family will lay out on our trampolean and watch the shower.

Today I woke up and started to whine. Lauren said, "Be quiet." I stopped, but I didn't know why I was whineing. It was weird! Anyway, today is a very nice and sunny day. So far I have enjoyed it. Well, I have to go. Bye.

Thursday, August 12th, three days before Kelly was scheduled to leave for camp, the girls and I went shopping for camp supplies. Standing in front of racks of shoes at a discount store, I sighed impatiently. "C'mon, Kelly," I said, watching her deliberate over yet another not-quite-suitable pair. "We've got to get you some sort of hiking boots to wear for camp. You leave in three days; do you see any you really like?"

Leslie spotted a pair of dark brown suede boots with fancy ties. "What about these?" she said.

"Pretty dressy for hiking, don't you think?" I commented, eyeing the fancy wide, sheer nylon ties that laced the tops.

"Oh, Mommy, I love them!" Kelly exclaimed. "Please? Can't I please try them on?"

I was too weary to argue, and there really wasn't much else to consider anyhow. "Okay, go ahead and try them on." It was love at first fit. "Okay, we'll get them. I just hope they work for camp and are still nice when school starts."

At home Kelly assembled the normal camp accouterments, then carefully laid out an outfit for a Mardi Gras party the camp had planned for one of the nights. "Do you think this'll be okay for Mardi Gras?" she asked, running her fingers through the shiny, metallic, multi-colored, grass skirt we had bought.

"I think you'll look fantastic with your Hawaiian-print bathing suit underneath and those beautiful leis around your neck. Your colored sandals even match."

Everything was laid out and ready to be packed. The beautiful brown suede boots stood at attention on the floor next to her bed. "I'm so excited to go to camp, Mommy. I hope I get to be with Susannah a lot."

A TABLE FOR TWO

Thursday, Agaust 12, 1993
Hi! Today has really been a good day! It is hot outside!
Tonight I am going to bed early because I have to get up at
5:00 in the morning! I am going to Philadelphia. It takes two
hours to get there! I go there for an M.R.I. Got to go, bye!

Since my friend Linda wouldn't be leaving until lunchtime on Friday, Rob and the girls made the trip to Philadelphia without me. I welcomed the break from the driving and all the treatment responsibility. Promptly at 5:30 a.m., they piled into the van and pulled out of the driveway. I knew the trip would be fun; Rob always managed to bring another dimension to the routine that had become fairly monotonous for Kelly and me. I figured they'd turn the radio to the golden oldies station and sing, laugh, and giggle most of the way down, once they were sufficiently awake.

The phone rang around 6:30 a.m. "Lisa," Rob said, "we're stuck on the turnpike behind a tractor-trailer accident and won't be able to arrive on time. I don't have the phone number, so could you call Radiology for us and tell them we'll be there as soon as possible? We've already been sitting here for 45 minutes."

"Everybody okay?"

"Yes, we're fine; trying to make the best of it. Well, gotta go. See ya."

Eight hours later when they returned home, everyone was tired but happy. They gave me a run-down of their trip: Leslie stayed with Kelly during her MRI, Rob and Lauren walked over to Franklin Field at the University of Pennsylvania, and then they all had lunch at McDonald's in the lobby of Children's Hospital. "It was good to remember that a year had gone by since we last ate there—much to be thankful for," Rob said.

All four of them dispersed into separate activities throughout the house. Kelly ran upstairs to do her daily diary—more impressed with the events of the night before than the mundane protocol of her treatment:

Friday, Agaust 13, 1993
Hi! I just got back from Philadelphia! It was a long ride!
Last night there was a thunderstorm! I woke up and woke
Leslie up, and we woke Lauren up. I woke up because Dad
was looking out the window, and I thought he was a burgalur.
We woke up at 3:37, and stayed up till 4:35 then went back
to sleep. Well, bye!

Kelly had been writing upstairs in her room when the phone rang around 4:00 p.m. "Let the answering machine get it," I called from my reclining position on the sofa where I had hoped to catch a little nap.

"Mommy," Kelly called from the top of the stairs where she had been listening to the message on the machine. "You'd better get it—it's the doctor."

I jumped up and rushed to the phone, hoping the caller wouldn't hang up. "Hello? This is Lisa Bair," I interrupted, breathlessly. "Sorry about the machine."

"Mrs. Bair, this is Dr. Molloy . . . "

My mind raced to place her—oh yes, the blonde woman who had led our brain tumor workshop. "Yes, I remember who you are."

"Dr. Janss is unavailable this weekend—"

She paused, and my emotions responded immediately to that familiar sympathetic tone, that hesitancy to go on. This wasn't going to be the regular callback to affirm a negative scan. I felt myself weakening.

"You might want to sit down," she said softly, ominously.

Numbly, I obeyed her.

"I'm really sorry to have to tell you this over the phone," she continued. "Normally I like to talk in person about these things, but since you're so far away . . . "

Involuntarily my body called forth every defense mechanism available to prepare for the shock, to shield me from the blow she was about to make. Like a fortress against the enemy, it built a wall of numbness around my thinking processes. I knew she was speaking, but her words ricocheted off in unrecognizable patterns.

"I'm sorry," I said, putting my hand to my forehead to rub the fog away. "I hear you talking. I just can't absorb what you're saying. C-could you repeat it, please?"

23.

"Kelly's MRI today revealed two new tumors, and one of them appears to be hemorrhaging," the doctor spoke slowly, deliberately. "She needs to go immediately to the hospital to be checked to see if she has enough platelets in her blood to deal with the bleeding."

Rob came through the garage door and into the kitchen where I was sitting. He took one look at my face and stopped in his tracks. I broke away from the conversation and spoke to him. The words spilled out of me like poison from a bottle turned upside down. "Kelly has two new tumors."

"*Two* of them?" I said, returning to Dr. Molloy. "Same location as her other one?"

"No, they're on either side of her head."

"And we have to do what?" My voice was dry and uneven, my hands trembly.

"Take her to the hospital. I'll call Hershey right now and let them know you're coming. We need to make sure the bleeding isn't endangering her. If her blood count is sufficient, she'll take care of the bleeding herself. But if not, she'll need a transfusion."

"Wait—" I said, struggling to sift through this information. "How big are these tumors? She has no symptoms at all of anything."

"They're located in what's called a 'silent' part of the brain; that's why she's been asymptomatic so far."

"A couple of weeks ago Kelly woke up in the middle of the night with a headache, and then in the morning couldn't read out loud to me from a book. Was that because of this?"

"It could well be. Anytime a child has a sudden headache, or wakes from a deep sleep like that with one, it's usually an indication of some sort of event. That's probably when she started to hemorrhage. We can't tell from the scan just exactly when she did, but we do need to check her."

Now the pieces began to fit. "So what do we do now?"

"We'd like you and your husband—you don't need to bring Kelly—to come to Philadelphia on Tuesday to discuss options."

I remembered Dr. Molloy saying at the workshop that some children have had two and three brain tumor resections. I shivered at the thought. "Will they want to operate again?"

"I'm very sorry—I know this is incredibly hard for you. But we really prefer to wait until you come here to talk with you in person."

I hung up the phone and looked at Rob.

"Kelly heard everything," he said, his face full of sorrow. "She was standing in the hall when she heard you tell me; then I found her sitting in the middle of the sofa in the living room—crying."

"Where is she now?"

"Upstairs."

We found the three girls sitting on the bed in Leslie's room, all crying and holding each other. Our arms went out to them, and they huddled under them. Scared, defeated, we could do nothing for a few moments but cry together.

"Kelly, the doctor said we have to go to the hospital to get a blood check," I said apologetically. "One of the tumors is bleeding a little, and you might need platelets."

Nobody protested. We left phone messages on the grandparents' answering machines and got in the car. We sat in stone-faced silence. After a few moments Rob spoke. "Kelly, we want you to know it's not just you against this cancer—it's all of us against this cancer. We're a family, and we're going to stick by you no matter what." Each of us added individual affirmations to that.

It took a half hour for us to reach the emergency entrance. Instructed to stay in the waiting area until Dr. Close arrived, we sat blankly, unable to involve ourselves even a little in the sitcoms that flashed from the TV screens suspended from the ceiling.

Soon we were back in a treatment room where Kelly received a blood test. Dr. Close arrived shortly thereafter. "Kelly, Kelly, Kelly," she said sympathetically, looking lovingly at her and taking hold of her hand. "Big, big bummer, huh?" Lying on the examining table, Kelly nodded silent agreement through the expression in her eyes.

"She was so excited and all set to go to camp on Sunday and everything," I said.

"Well, Kelly, if your blood's okay and your examination is okay, it's fine with me for you to go to camp. I'm the camp doctor, by the way, so if you have any problems, I'll be right there to help you."

"You'd really let her go?" I asked, incredulous.

"Sure, if she really wants to, and if Dr. Molloy agrees with me that it'll be okay. How 'bout it, Kiddo? Do you want to go?"

Kelly smiled hopefully. "Yes!"

After examining her, Dr. Close sent Kelly back to her sisters and told them to go outside on the big front lawn and get some fresh air. She shepherded us into a secluded hallway. "Dr. Molloy told me the tumors are fairly significant in size, but because of where they're located, they still have room to grow before they'll start causing symptoms. I live five minutes from the camp, so you can rest assured she'll be looked after, and we'll be available should she need us." She made a note on her clipboard. "I'm going to call Dr. Molloy once I receive the results of her blood work, and then I'll let you know what our decision is. If you haven't eaten dinner yet, why don't you do that while you wait. It's going to be at least 45 minutes 'til we get the results."

We joined the girls outside where they had picked Queen Anne's lace and were putting it in their hair and behind Kelly's ear. "You guys hungry?" Rob asked.

We had nearly finished eating when Dr. Close came by our table. "Good news, Kelly," she said smiling. "Your blood's fine, you don't need a transfusion, and the word is 'go' for camp!" She scribbled something on a pad and handed it to me. "Here's my home phone number. Please call me if you need me."

Returning home on Route 283, we had a transformation of spirit in the back seats. While Rob's and my faces were hopelessly somber, *giggling*—of all things—started to bubble up among the sisters, and then the strains of a camp song: *I found a little baby bumblebee; won't my mama be so proud of me. . . .* They continued singing it over and over, each new verse a more hysterical unison. The more they sang, the more they laughed.

I looked at Rob in sheer disbelief. *What happened?*

He looked at me. *I don't know, but don't break the spell.* It was holy anesthesia, coping balm for the soul. When we returned home, Kelly took out her diary:

> *Hi. The hospital called with the results of the M.R.I. My cancer is back! I went to Hershey Hospital to get a blood test and my blood is good. Before we left for Hershey my family all cryed. Crying really releaved me! But I am still a little scarde! I'm looking up to God to get us through this again! I burst into tears as soon as I herd the news!*
>
> *Now I am fine I think. Linda left today. For camp I got shoes that are swade. They are so neat! I try not to think about my cancer but it's kind of hard not to. Well I have to go to bed, I'm tired. Good night. Bye.*

> *Saturday, Agaust 14, 1993*
> *Hi. Today was a fun day. I made three neckleses and I went to the rag shop today with my grandparents. Tomarrow I am*

*going to camp! I'll go in the afternoon. Leslie and Lauren are
going to South Carolinea with my other grandparents tomarrow. I have to go. Bye.*

In some respects it seemed incomprehensible to me that, in
the middle of such anguishing news, we would split as a family two days later for an entire week. If Kelly had not wanted to
go to camp so badly, we would never have been able to leave
her, and Lauren and Leslie would have stayed home. As for the
two of us, we had declined the trip to South Carolina months
before, knowing that Kelly would be at camp and that a slight
fever could hospitalize her.

We gave early morning good-bye hugs to Lauren and Leslie.
"Don't forget to call us right away after you talk to the doctors
in Philadelphia," they urged.

"We won't forget."

"Bye, Kelly," they each said, hugging her tightly. "Have a
great time at camp. We'll write you!"

Kelly smiled. As much as she loved being with her sisters,
she also relished being able to make an independent trip of her
own. It made her feel grown up, something the youngest child
always struggles to feel.

After church it was time to take Kelly to her camp, 45 minutes away. The knots in our stomachs tightened as we drove
slowly into the campground. Letting her come to camp was not
our first choice, knowing how precarious her health was and
how bleak her future might be. But we were determined to
serve her every wish and to keep our course as normal as possible. What else was there to do?

Approaching the last turn, we saw the registration pavilion.
My unspoken mother-concerns welled up in my heart: *Camp
can be tough on normal, healthy children. What if she makes no
friends and gets desperately homesick? What if she needs to talk
deeply about what she's feeling, and no one is sensitive to that?
What if she starts showing symptoms of her tumors?* I felt tearful,
but I could not, would not, lose my composure.

Our van came to a stop. Painfully I opened the car door. "Kelly!" came a voice out of the group of people stationed at the pavilion. I turned to see Michelle, our child-life specialist friend, emerge from the crowd and start running toward us, arms outstretched. She went straight for Kelly and threw her arms around her. "Kelly! I'm so glad you're here! We're going to have so much fun together this week! Guess what? I get to be your counselor."

There was no way a kid could feel sad after a greeting like that, and no way an anxiety-ridden mother could keep her tears of gratitude inside. Later, after Kelly got registered and Rob and she were walking hand-in-hand ahead of us, I leaned closer to Michelle. "We've had a rather emotional weekend—"

"I know," she said kindly. "Dr. Close briefed us this morning. I'm really sorry. We'll take good care of her here—don't worry."

Driving out of the camp, Rob lost his control. "This is one of the hardest things I've ever done," he said, his voice breaking, "knowing what we know, and just leaving her there."

As we stepped into our house, loneliness overwhelmed us. Even Tucker, without the stimulation of the children, greeted us briefly, then went to lie down. Grief filled our hearts. What would we be told on Tuesday in Philadelphia? What kind of dreaded options would we have to consider?

The following afternoon while I was cooking supper on the stove, Rob came over beside me. "Look," he said. "You won't believe what I found." He flipped open a complimentary insurance calendar that had arrived in the mail that day. Turning to the month of November, he placed the picture in front of me. Standing in a field of golden, waist-high wheat was a little girl Kelly's size and build, wearing a hat, a few blonde wisps of hair visible underneath. Her profile was so close to that of Kelly's that it could have been her twin. It was an ethereal picture—misty and hauntingly beautiful. Looking at it tortured us with thoughts of her—out of reach, out of touch, perhaps out of our future.

The next day at noon we drove for Philadelphia. There were prayers ascending from the lips of countless church people and close friends. Still, my anxiety was high, and neither of us looked forward to our talk with the doctors. I also dreaded the possibility of running into Cindy and Chris King. Tuesday was oncology clinic day at the hospital, and, while it was unlikely that our appointment would coincide with theirs, it was not improbable. We had been teammates in our emotional struggles, comrades on a nearly identical time line. Now one of us was splitting off course into the dreaded hazard of the journey: recurrence of cancer. How could we break the balloon of hope we had held high for each other? And how could they bear the agony of what we were facing—feeling sorry for us, as well as afraid that it might happen to them?

We emerged from the elevators. When I turned the corner, I saw her sitting at the end of the hall. I couldn't avoid an encounter. In spite of my reluctance to see her, I had missed her. It had been months since we had seen each other. "Cindy!" I called.

She broke into a broad smile and rushed down the hall, arms open wide. She held me, then broke away and looked around. "Where's Kelly?"

"At camp," I said slowly. "We're here for a conference with the doctors." I paused, not wanting to pour pain into her dark, searching eyes. "Kelly's MRI on Friday revealed two new tumors."

Her face full of sadness, she gathered both of us in her arms and held us close. "Dear Father in heaven," she prayed, "surround this precious family with your sovereign wisdom and healing strength. Help them to know that you are in their midst—that this situation is in your hands, for your glory. Give them the comfort they need—"

Her prayer was cut off when Chris and his younger sister Faith came running to join us. "Where's Kelly?" they asked eagerly, stretching their necks to get a view of the waiting room area.

"She's at camp this week," I said as cheerfully as I could. I decided to let Cindy relate the other news.

Dr. Janss found us in the waiting room. Without hesitation, she, too, embraced us tightly. Kissing my cheek, she whispered, "I'm so sorry." Her manner, as always, was soothing and restorative.

We sat around a table with her, another doctor, and a social worker. Dr. Janss pulled Kelly's MRI scans from a huge envelope. Placing them in front of us, she pointed to the two new tumors we had known about, both larger than we had imagined. Then she pointed to two pea-sized beginning tumors at two other locations. I knew immediately that surgery was not one of the options and that the cancer had spread hopelessly out of control. I felt a horrible heat rush through my body, mixed with a bizarre, cool sense of relief that we didn't have to endure more surgery. "Do you think it's gone into her spine, as well?" I asked, recalling the tendency of ependymomas to seed into the spinal as well as cranial fluids.

"Most likely," she said. "We can't know for sure without doing a spinal tap, but my guess is, it has.

"There are several things we can do," Dr. Janss continued gently, "but you need to understand that everything we're suggesting will only lengthen her time, not cure her. There's nothing we can do at this point to cure her." She paused to let the information sink in, then went on to describe two different, more intensive, chemotherapy options. "You have to choose what you and Kelly feel most comfortable with. You may decide not to do any more treatment at all. We suggest you talk to her about it and then decide."

There was only one burning question on our hearts. "I know you probably don't like to answer this," I said weakly, "but if we were to choose no further treatment, how much time do you think she'd have left?"

The question was inevitable, Dr. Janss knew. "I don't think it will be less than a month," she said carefully. Hesitating, unwilling to have us depend too much on her response, she added, "But I don't think it will be longer than several months."

The brevity of the time span jolted me.

"If you're wanting to do something together as a family," she continued, "now's the time to do it—while Kelly's still symptom-free."

"What kinds of symptoms do you anticipate she'll have, based on where these tumors are located?" Rob asked.

"It's hard to say exactly. There's definitely a possibility of seizures, and her speech and hearing could be affected—headaches, eyesight problems, walking. We'll be in close touch with Hershey as she progresses through this." She looked at us tenderly and placed her hand on Rob's arm. "You need to know, above all else—even if you choose no further treatment—that we're not going to abandon you. Our goal is to keep Kelly as comfortable as possible."

She had spoken the words we needed to hear. The whole meeting, including the information and attitudes from everyone there, seemed filled with God's caring presence and comfort. We talked about it afterwards, while we strolled the streets and university commons of Philadelphia for an hour or so before we felt like returning home. But what would we tell Lauren and Leslie and our families? Should we give the kids the opportunity to fly home if they wanted to be with us? Would it be better if we flew them home first, then told them? How would we tell Kelly? Who, we wondered, held the instruction manual for something like this?

That evening we stopped by Rob's parents' home to tell them the news. Punched with the reality of what they heard, they sat with us, their faces filled with sadness. They had some unfinished business on their minds, however, and wanted to make their intentions clear.

"We'd like, more than anything in the world, for your whole family to go to Disney World." It had been their tradition to take each of their grandchildren, in the spring of their third-grade year, to Orlando for a five-day vacation. Kelly, the youngest of the grandchildren, was the only one who had not yet gone. We had all wondered, ever since the onset of her ill-ness, whether or not she'd be able to go.

"I don't know," I said. "It's scary to think of her going on a trip with the kind of medical problems she has."

"But Dr. Janss said that if we're going to do anything as a family, we'd better do it now," Rob urged.

Then an idea occurred to me. "I've heard that if you go through the Make-A-Wish Foundation, you can stay at a place where medical treatment is quickly accessible, and there are waiting-in-line exceptions made for ill children."

We decided to investigate the option. But before that, there remained the dreaded task of communicating the news to our children and my side of the family in South Carolina. Kelly, we decided, didn't need to be told until she came home. The other two, we knew, would not rest until they heard.

24.

Our hearts beat heavily as we dialed their number in South Carolina. We knew the entire clan waited anxiously to hear from us. My father picked up the phone. "Dad, could we have some time alone with the girls?" Quickly, Lauren and Leslie picked up separate extensions; their cousins were herded into another room.

"What did the doctor say?" they asked anxiously.

"Well, we had a good meeting," Rob started carefully, his subsequent pause gaping like a canyon between us and them. We wanted to be present with them and shoulder their pain with our bodies, but if we waited to tell them until they got home, they would sense the worst, left alone with the comfortless arms of their imaginations. We had to tell them now, and we prayed desperately about how to do it. "But things don't look so good," he continued. "It appears that God—" He swallowed hard. "God—may be telling the angels to get Kelly's room ready in heaven."

The news settled in silence; then we heard Leslie crying. "The whole family prayed together at breakfast," Lauren said, her own voice choking. "Everyone was crying."

We talked at length about what Dr. Janss had said, and then suggested the idea of a trip to Disney World. "Would you guys want to go?" Rob asked.

The mere suggestion of the trip sparked some enthusiasm and began to lighten the conversation slightly. "If you two want to come home now, we'll let you," I said. "Or if you want to stay, that's okay, and you may call when you feel you need to." After some deliberation with them, and a conversation with my parents, we agreed that it would be easiest just to finish out the vacation as planned.

The days following were unmatched by anything we had experienced in our 19 years of marriage. Our childless house and the kids' quiet, neat bedrooms continually reminded us of the impending absence we all faced. We parented from afar every moment of each day, making mental assessments of where we imagined our children to be emotionally. What was Kelly thinking? Did she wonder how our meeting had gone? Was she feeling well? Was she busy enough to keep her mind off her fears?

We sent her carefully chosen cards which captured our deep feeling for her and which expressed some of what we wished we could give her in person. Often we cried as we wrote them and hugged them to our hearts before we put them in the mail.

Oddly, we didn't hear from her, in spite of the postcards I had addressed for her to send to us. Midweek, Pastor Tom came over to take a hike with Rob, and his wife Dori brought their two sons, at my invitation, to jump on the trampoline.

Upon seeing them, Tucker came back to life again, racing around the yard and barking for them to throw the ball. *Kids again! Finally some action!* he must have thought. I felt it, too. "It's really good to have some kids around—this week's been awfully quiet and lonely," I told Dori.

She looked at me kindly. "I was surprised—today we got a postcard from Kelly."

"You got a postcard? She hasn't even written to *us* yet! What did she say? I want to know every word."

Dori recounted what Kelly had written as best she could. "She's having a great time. I'm sorry—I should have brought it along. I'll see that you get it."

Friday night our loneliness fermented into fear. The next day we would pick Kelly up at camp, and, while we missed her desperately, we dreaded it terribly. We prayed for wisdom for the way to tell her, for comfort for her. Ma-Ma and Pop-Pop had asked to ride along, so when morning finally arrived, we began the trip, feeling every painful quarter-mile of the distance.

We drove into the camp to the place where we had dropped her off the week before. A big charter bus transporting children from Philadelphia blocked the pavilion. My eyes passionately searched the mob of kids in myriad colors milling around it. Like a shepherd looking for a lost sheep, I finally spotted her white hat, threw open the car door and rushed to meet her. I tapped her from behind, and she turned to greet me. She never looked so beautiful or as happy to see me.

Reunited with any of the girls after a week-long camp experience was always a sweet experience—we felt heightened appreciation for them and they for us. But the sweetness of this reunion pierced me. Burdened with the knowledge I held within me, I held her smallness against me, hoping to give the pain no room to breathe.

In the van on the way home, Ma-Ma kept Kelly occupied with questions. Obviously exhausted from the week, Kelly sank back into the seat to rest her head. She had had a wonderful time, she said. Stories slowly unraveled. With each pause in the conversation I kept bracing for her to ask about our meeting with the doctors. We had planned to wait until we got home to talk. Fortunately, she didn't ask. While I wanted to hear of her good time, the pain in my heart was excruciating, pressing against my chest like a great wall of dammed water.

At home, after we said good-bye to Ma-Ma and Pop-Pop, Kelly asked to watch TV. I stayed with her, ready to absorb any story or concern that seeped out of her, waiting for cues as to when to launch the inevitable discussion. I looked at Rob as he went outside to attend to some yard work. We had agreed I'd let him know the moment she asked about it.

"May I watch with you?" I asked, sitting in the swivel chair and reaching for her to sit on my lap. Wearily, she climbed up on me and laid her head on my shoulder. I stroked her back and savored the softness of her hair under my chin, breathing in her scent. As close as I held her, I could not bridge the great valley that seemed to be between us.

My thoughts were far from the characters on the TV screen—until my blank gaze was sliced through as one teenage boy told another that his lizard had died. "He's just a lizard," he said laughing. "Who cares about a silly old lizard, anyway?" But his joking quickly subsided as his face revealed the affection and grief he held inside.

It was light Saturday TV fare, comedy for some, but all too life-intense for me. It triggered something in Kelly, too, because she looked up at me and finally asked: "What did the doctors say about me on Tuesday?"

"Do you want to talk about it now, or after the show's over?" I asked.

"After it's over," she said, snuggling her head back into my shoulder.

The show ended five minutes later, and she moved to our L-shaped sofa and sprawled out on her back, exhausted. I summoned Rob in from the outside, and then stretched out on my stomach on the other part of the sofa, my head next to hers.

Kelly turned her head to observe my face. "You seem upset," she said softly.

"I am," I said honestly. There was no way to hide, no way to conceal the pain. Nobody on earth could have prepared me for such a moment. Rob came in then and sat down on the swivel chair. "We had a good meeting with Dr. Janss. She said to tell you she loves you and misses you, and you'll be glad to know they don't want to do any more surgery." Kelly looked relieved. "But they want you to decide whether you want to have more intensive chemotherapy, because the chemo you're on isn't working anymore."

She listened intently, trying to piece together this information with the pain she read in our faces.

"Kelly, none of the medicines can make the tumors go away. They can help slow down their growth for a while, but that's all." I paused, knowing I needed to say the word, clarify the truth, come out from behind the tree. "Unless God heals you—which he could, we don't know—you need to know that you might . . . die."

I had spoken gently, looking for all the anesthesia in the world, anything to cushion the impact of the fatal word, but there was none to be found. It hung on its own, stark and painful, dangling on the edge of a cliff.

I urgently searched her face for a response, aching to soothe the agony I had inflicted. Sober-faced, she knit her eyebrows, absorbing my words, saying nothing.

"Kelly," Rob said, "we want it to be your decision whether you get more chemo and have longer to live, or whether you decide not to, and just enjoy the time you do have, feeling pretty good."

"I don't want any more chemo," she said flatly.

Rob moved to the sofa. "This is a very tough time," he said tenderly, stroking her legs. "But we're going to be here to help you the best we can. And so will Lauren and Leslie. We've already talked to them on the phone, and they can't wait to see you tomorrow."

She looked at us briefly, then turned onto her side, her face away from us, and promptly fell asleep. We stroked her back for a few minutes, then let her sleep. "She's so exhausted," I whispered. "Sleep is probably the best way for her to cope with this right now."

Two hours later, Kelly awoke. I remembered from my own childhood the weary disorientation of being home after a week of camp. *What have I done?* I thought. *An eight-year-old comes home from a great camp experience, and her mother announces to her that she's going to die.* I ached to patch it all up—this twisted underside of the tapestry.

"Kelly," I said after dinner, noticing her quiet mood. "We don't want you to be depressed all by yourself. We want to talk about things with you. Are you okay?" *Okay? What am I saying? How would I answer a question like that? Sure, Mom, I'm okay— I just got home from camp and learned I'm going to die.*

We kept trying to open the door to more conversation. It's what you're supposed to do, or so we thought. We had read case studies of parents who refused to acknowledge or accept their child's impending death. The articles all concurred that it's better to get it out in the open. *Who's got the rule book to something like this?*

But Kelly quickly closed the door to more conversation. "I know you want to talk about it, but it makes me too sad. Can we please not talk about it?"

We had weighed her down enough, and she, for her own emotional survival, had found her own coping mechanisms. We got the message loud and clear, realizing that we needed to talk more than she did. "Okay," we said apologetically. "We're sorry. But will you remember that if you ever do want to talk about it, you can bring it up anytime?"

"Yes."

Soon we were playing table games, living in and trying to enjoy the moment—alive and together.

25.

Living with a child who is expected to die is some of the sweetest and cruelest living there is. Invisibly a barrier forms between you, and no matter how long or how tightly you hold her, or how deeply you look into her eyes, you haven't really reached her. And so while part of you wants to quickly end this unbearably torturous interim, another part keeps longing to hold her again, to apprehend with eyes and heart for all of time, to pin her down, bring her safely to your side, keep enough of her before the looming, incomprehensible departure.

There is little solace. The process cannot be quickened—nor can she be contained or apprehended, and there is never enough of her to satisfy. The journey will not be hastened or stopped by onlookers who grab at the hems of those traveling the path.

Mixed with all our wrenching emotion was our desire to keep life as routine as possible, to avoid turning our home and lives into a maudlin holding ground. Young children, we reasoned, live more in the present. Without compromising the open communication we so highly valued in our family, we tried hard to keep from Kelly the weight of our adult hearts. We knew the return of her sisters would help immensely.

A TABLE FOR TWO

Sunday night we went to a local restaurant to have supper with my parents and Lauren and Leslie, who had just returned from South Carolina. My father called us from his car phone to tell us the approximate time they would pull into the restaurant parking lot. They arrived before we did, and my mother commented later that the sight of her grand-daughter—a small, compellingly winsome, white-hatted figure seated behind us in our approaching van—was almost more than she could bear.

The reunion was sweet for the three sisters, and the chains around our hearts loosened momentarily as the three of them shared all about their week away from each other, resumed their routine bantering, and talked about the opening of school. For a few ensuing days, things felt refreshingly normal around the house. But that was precisely the problem. Things *weren't* normal, and we had yet to talk about it together as a family.

After several days, Rob and I agreed we needed to break open the subject again, this time at the dinner table. "You know, all of us have been acting as if nothing is wrong in this house," Rob said. "It's great that there's an atmosphere of happiness around here, but we're probably going through one of the toughest ordeals any family ever has to endure. And we need to talk about it." There was a look of *oh, no* in each of their faces. "How are we all feeling?"

Silence. I decided to break the ice and go first. "I feel really sad most of the time, and sometimes I hide my tears. And then I hurt for you guys, wondering if you're doing the same thing and whether you might be afraid to talk to us about it because you know we're already suffering."

"We hurt, too," Leslie said. "But it's not like this is our favorite subject to talk about."

"We know," Rob said. "This is nobody's favorite subject. But it's what we're being given to deal with. So we have to deal with it."

"I think about it all the time," Lauren said. "But it's not good to dwell on it, is it?"

"We're not asking any of you to dwell on it," I said. "We just want it to be out in the open, that's all. Then we can get on with the living that we need to do."

"Kelly, all of us feel very deeply for you," Rob said. "We wish more than anything that you wouldn't have to go through this. But most of all, we don't want you to have to go through this alone, and if we don't ever talk about it we all start to feel isolated in our pain. Do you?"

"What does 'isolated' mean?" she asked, stirring her vegetables with her fork.

"It means you feel all alone."

"I do sometimes."

The conversation continued for only a little while longer, but there was a noticeable change in the climate among us. Ever so slightly, we had lightened the burden on each of our shoulders by sharing it. As for Kelly, who could honestly know the depth of her feelings? She was being required to forge a path no one had walked before her. We could only watch, helplessly, from the edges.

In light of the circumstances, I gave myself permission to enter her confidences; I searched the diary she had received for her birthday. But there were no entries—not since her trip to camp. Had she stopped writing out of a sense of defeat?

One morning a few days later, I found Kelly in her room making necklaces. "Lauren wants to go to the Rag Shop. Wanna go along?" I asked. She shook her head no. "Are you sure? It's your favorite store."

She sat on the floor not looking up, intricately stringing tiny colorful beads on a thin strand. "Are you wanting to finish your necklace, or are you depressed?" I asked.

She paused, then said quietly, "Both."

"Do you feel like talking about it?"

"Not really."

"You know I'm here if you do feel like it."

"I know."

I walked down the steps, my heart splitting. The more it

tore, the more it bled. Enraged with the helplessness I felt, I feared even God wasn't doing the job I felt he should in ministering to her. I felt locked out of her life, incapable of helping her pack emotionally for the most significant and grueling journey of her life. I went to the bathroom, locked the door, and released my tears. "I can't reach her, God!" I cried as quietly as I could into a towel. "Please, please . . . help her. Don't leave her alone in this! You *have* to help her deal with this. I simply don't know what to do."

Within a few days, another entry appeared in Kelly's journal. I read it with mixed relief. Either she couldn't plumb the depth of her feeling, by virtue of her age and the extreme pathos of her situation, or she found it understandably more bearable not to think about it:

> *Thursday, Agaust 26, 1993*
> *Hi! Today is so nice outside. Sorry I didn't write for a pretty long time! I was to busy. Yesterday I got a lockit for myself. It is so neat! I am putting my sisters' and my dog's pictshure in it. I can't find Leslie's pictshure in a small enouph size to fit in my lockit. Well, got to go. Bye.*

Soon there was little time to dwell on feelings. We kicked into a whirlwind of planning and preparation. We had contacted the Make-A-Wish Foundation, and they were due to arrive in a day or two. "It's our policy to hear—straight from the child—what her wish is," they had said. "So be sure to ask Kelly to think about two wishes: her first, and a second, if we can't, for some reason, make the first wish come true."

Meanwhile, Rob and I went to Hershey to meet with the nurse practitioner, a social worker, and Dr. Close. We wanted advice on how to care for Kelly in the days ahead, particularly in regard to our anticipated trip to Florida.

"I'm going to prescribe Dylantin for her today," Dr. Close said. "It's an anti-seizure medication. I'll also give you about four or five levels of headache medicine."

"What if she has symptoms, such as a headache, and none of this helps?" I asked.

"If she goes that dramatically from no symptoms to something that severe, then we'll know that things are happening pretty fast."

"Exactly how does death occur in a case like this?" I asked, recoiling from the sound of my own question. But I needed information, coping strategies.

"Pressure," she responded. "The brain only has so much room in it, and as the tumors enlarge and crowd it, pressure is put on the brain stem, which controls breathing and heart rate." She paused to wait for any further questions, then pulled out a calendar. "I hear you're planning a trip to Disney World. I suggest you plan to go the second full week in September. Don't go the week school starts—Kelly needs to acclimate emotionally to the new school year. If you wait until the third week, you might regret it."

A few days later, two cheerful Make-A-Wish volunteers arrived, and our family gathered in the living room to talk with them. We knew Kelly definitely wanted to go to Disney World, but, as per our instructions from Make-A-Wish, we told her to think real hard about any other wish she had. She had looked forward to her "coming of age" trip with Ma-Ma and Pop-Pop for several years, and we simply didn't question that would be her wish.

"Kelly," the friendly volunteer started, "are you prepared to tell us your wish?"

"Yes," she said expectantly.

"Good. We're ready. What is your wish?"

"I'd like to go to Hawaii."

HAWAII???!!! It was all I could do to contain my shock. "I thought you wanted to go to Disney World," I said as evenly and respectfully as possible.

"I do, but I also want to see Hawaii."

"Is it because we watched that TV show last night about those teenagers in Hawaii?"

The volunteer rescued us. "Kelly, if you want to go to Disney World as much as Hawaii, I think Disney World might be a better choice. We had an older teenager go to Hawaii once for her wish, but there's really not much for children your age to do there. In Disney World, there's tons of stuff to do, and they have a special village where the Wish children stay. What do you think?"

"Okay, Disney World's fine," Kelly answered.

"Are you sure?"

"Yes. I really want to go there, too. That was my other wish."

The volunteers scrambled to make arrangements for the trip during the week we had requested. Meanwhile, I made phone calls to the school to alert them to Kelly's medical situation.

Wednesday night, September 1st, our church held a healing service for the community. Clad in a soft, cotton, T-shirt dress with wide, blue and white stripes, Kelly sat quietly in the sanctuary. "Tonight," Pastor David began, "whether or not it occurs in the form we request it, there will be healing of some kind in the lives of all who seek it, because Jesus and healing are one and the same."

At the invitation, our family went to the altar with Kelly where she received the second anointing of her young life. We all laid hands on her and prayed for God's purpose to be manifest in her.

Coming out of the church that night, we had mixed feelings. Perhaps God *would* heal her after all. How would we ever know? At the moment, she was feeling better than she had in months. "It's hard to know how to pray," I told Rob. "Are we supposed to demand a healing, 'name it and claim it,' or resign and prepare ourselves for her death?"

"I just don't feel like God wants us to beg him like that," Rob said. "He knows our desires and the agony of our hearts about all this."

"I feel the same way. In one sense I feel that if we kicked and screamed about it, God might honor our prayers—but it would be like King Hezekiah when he pleaded for more years and got them, and they were the worst of his life. Do you ever get the sense that God's got his own agenda here, and we're to cooperate with it—the 'not my will but yours' kind of prayer?"

I had no way of knowing exactly how God was ministering strength to Kelly. But I did notice a considerable improvement in her since my prayer in the bathroom and then the healing service. She seemed to have risen to a new resolve, enjoying the activities she liked to do. She had an uncharacteristic quantity of fresh energy because it had been a long time since her last chemotherapy.

Her normal zest for life seemed to return as well. One afternoon I heard her in the midst of a little friendly bickering in the kitchen with one of her sisters, after which she stomped off in a feisty huff, swung around the banister to go upstairs, and shouted boisterously, "Oh, just let me go to Disney World and then I'll die!"

Whenever we found time to be alone, Rob and I talked about the stages we'd likely enter with Kelly's progressive illness. He planned how he would set up a bed in the dining room for her. I focused on how to medicate her, who to call for hospice care, getting a pager to wear in case something happened at school and I wasn't available.

We read case studies given to us by our social worker and written by parents who went through the dying process with a child. We cried through the painful reading of them. But it was immensely helpful information we desperately needed.

One afternoon I was lying on the couch in the living room thinking about all this when Lauren came in. "Mom," she said softly, lowering her voice even further when she knew she had my attention. "Um, if—if Kelly dies, do you think it'd be okay for me to have her teddy bear?"

My heart went out to Lauren. I had been so caught up in my own grief that I was touched and relieved to see her acting upon her own. But she had her eye on the most coveted item in Kelly's possession, and I couldn't immediately decide. "I think we're all going to need him," I said. "But if you'd like to keep him in your room, that'd be okay with me."

Days later, Rob and I had questions for which we wanted specific answers—answers which could come only from Kelly. We called her to come into the living room and talk for a while. She sat down on the floor with a displeased moan. We had that "look" about us, and we had interrupted her necklace-making.

"Kelly," I said. "You know that God could still heal you. We're always open to that possibility. But we have to consider some things in case he decides to take you straight to heaven."

"Like what?" she sighed, rolling her eyes.

"Like—if you were to die, would you rather be in the hospital, or here at home?"

Her response was immediate. "Here at home."

"And, even though you would be in heaven with Jesus and wouldn't even be in your body anymore, do you have any feeling about where you'd want us to bury it?" I hated this question, not knowing if an eight-year-old should even be asked or could possibly grasp this.

"In that cemetery near your school, Daddy," she said. Landisville Mennonite Cemetery was the only one she'd every visited—the burial site of her great-grandparents and several other relatives with whom she was not acquainted.

"Did you know there's a cemetery right beside our development?" Rob asked. We had barely known it existed until we started thinking about all this, so well-hidden from the road it was. We had already imagined ourselves needing to visit it often, talking grief walks there with Tucker.

Her eyes lit up. "Oh yeah! That one."

"That one's okay?"

"Yeah. And put my teddy in the casket with me."

We were getting straight answers, which was good. But now we had a conflict over Lauren's request to have the teddy bear and Kelly's need to have one small item of tangible comfort. She couldn't comprehend not being a feeling person in the casket. I opted to let that one go for further consideration. On to other topics while she was cooperating.

"Kelly," I asked, "you know your dream of Jesus eating with you at the table for two? Can you remember back and tell me absolutely everything else you recall about that dream?"

She spoke as if it were still as fresh as the morning she recounted it to me two-and-a-half months before. "Well, there were other people eating around us."

This was new information. "Other people?"

"Yes. A lot of them. Only my table had a beautiful soft glow on it."

"Were other people at tables for two also?"

"I'm not sure, but there were other tables."

"What did your table look like?"

"There were two white plates that had raised designs around the edges—one for Jesus and one for me—but there wasn't any food on them."

"Any knives, forks, or spoons?"

"Nothing else. Except in the center of the table there was this pretty clear-glass candlestick shaped like this—" she drew her hands up in a tapered fashion—"and it was lit."

"Anything else you can remember?"

She shook her head. "Can I please go now and finish my necklaces?" We had exhausted our informant. Enough for the day.

Several days later Rob came home and sat down in the rocking chair across from where I was writing a letter. "Lisa, you won't believe this," he said quietly, holding an envelope in his hand and pulling out a large slip of paper. He passed it to me and I quickly saw it was a check. My mouth fell open at the amount. "It's from the school community. They want to fund our trip to Disney World."

As with other gifts extended toward us, we were deeply warmed, humbled, and unable to restrain our tears in response. But this one was extravagant, and I didn't know what to do. "How can we accept this?" I said. "This is enough to fund two or three children's families going to Disney World."

"They wanted us to have it. We'll return the trip amount to Make-A-Wish, and Harriet suggested we buy a cam corder with it also. Then we pray about what to do with the rest. Perhaps we can contribute to the Four Diamonds Fund. They've covered nearly everything our insurance hasn't."

The fall term had only been in progress three days before we had to pull the girls out of school for our trip to Florida. We had primed Kelly's new third-grade teacher, Mrs. Charles, and had given her medical information about what might transpire under her supervision, but, so far, all was well.

The school day came to a close on that warm, bright Friday afternoon of September 10th, and in the bus line Kelly caught up with her beloved first-grade teacher, Mrs. Neff. "Kelly, you have a great trip, you hear?" she said, giving her a hug. "We'll be counting on you to tell us all about it when you get back!"

Kelly took her hand and held it tightly. "I'm not letting you go—because I'm taking you with me," she said with a mischievous smile.

"You are? Great!"

"I haven't told my mom yet, but I can easily fit you in my suitcase."

"What time should I be ready?"

They both chuckled at this plan; then Kelly's line of children began to board the bus. Kelly still didn't let go of her hand, and Mrs. Neff followed along beside her. It was a picture poignantly and indelibly printed in Nancy Neff's mind when, up on the first step, Kelly paused to look deeply into her teacher's eyes. "Well," she said softly, reluctantly releasing her hand. "I guess I have to say good-bye now."

It would be their last moment together on earth.

26.

Tuesday, September 14, 1993
I am in the plane, seat number twenty-two F (right win-
dow). I feel so excited!
WE ARE UP!
My ears are weird! I miss my dog Tucker!

Kelly's eyes were bright with wonder as she gazed into the expansive sky and marveled at the diminutive landscape below. Rob, seated next to her, shared in her excitement, describing the plane's ascent and pointing out the Maryland shoreline below. I was grateful for his enthusiasm for flying; it made up for my lack of it and helped Kelly's first air experience to be more positive.

"Oh please," she begged. "May I take some pictures of the clouds?" I handed her the camera, but, after snapping several pictures, she leaned back into her seat. Her face took on a familiar look.

"Are you woozy?" I asked. She closed her eyes and nodded ever so slightly. A stewardess brought her a pillow, and Kelly proceeded to sleep for the next hour.

At the Orlando airport friendly volunteers held up a sign: "Give Kids the World welcomes Kelly Bair!" The connecting arm for Disney Wish children, GKTW proceeded to roll out the red carpet for us, complete with a rental car, beautiful two-bedroom villa, and free passes to special events. It was more hospitality than I could emotionally take. My eyes watered with each new gesture of care. We'd had over a year of stress and chronic heartsickness and a month of acute grief. Now we were so weary from trying to get ready for this five-day trip that I could barely assimilate such extravagant treatment.

The kids were delighted with the hospitality T-shirts given them, along with free souvenirs and buttons. They bubbled excitedly about our beautiful accommodations, marveled at the refrigerator stocked with snacks, and quickly staked claims on their preferred beds.

Our first evening there we were given tickets to Wild Bill's, a country-western dinner show. While waiting for us to get ready to go, the kids clicked on the TV. A news bulletin came on. "Mom, Dad! Come here quick!" they called. We went to the living room and saw the screen flash information on yet another tourist shooting in the Orlando area. As before, a rental car had been apprehended by terrorists. "Do you think it's safe to go out?" they asked.

I kept watching the screen, a sick feeling rising inside me. How many tourist murders had there been now, I wondered— four? Five? Rob didn't seem to be intimidated by this. "The place is jammed with tourists, guys. I don't think we need to be overly concerned."

That evening we parked our rental car at Wild Bill's. I tried not to concern the girls, but I did find myself looking suspiciously over my shoulder now and then. Once through the entrance, we came into a huge courtyard-type area where people were sipping lemonade and looking at Wild Bill memorabilia. Suddenly I felt something in my back, heard a shot and a whooping holler, and whipped around to see the costumed Wild Bill himself crying with glee, "Gotcha!" He danced off with his aluminum cap gun to find another unsuspecting dame while I stood there, unsmiling, my heart in my throat. Tonight, it just wasn't funny.

The next morning our family awoke raring to go—all except Kelly. "I have a bad headache," she said, slumping back into her pillow. My enthusiasm plummeted. Anxiety rose. I could picture us needing to turn around and go back home. I gave her the lowest level headache medicine, and, while she continued to rest, the others went for breakfast.

Within 20 minutes she vomited, then asked, "Can we go now?"

"Are you sure?"

"Yes. Can we get some breakfast?"

Kelly and I walked over to the dining hall to join the others. The place, a gingerbread house ornately decorated with huge plaster candies, was bustling with music and conversation and sizzling with color. Disney characters mingled with the crowd and signed autographs while families like ours chose food, cafeteria-style.

It was a cheerful place, and sweet hospitality for the soul. I couldn't stop the tears, so lavish was the healing love being poured upon us. I caught my reflection in the mirror and, for a fleeting moment, understood the mercy of this wonderful place toward people like the emotionally eroded image I saw in the glass.

An orientation director made one thing clear in the meeting that followed breakfast: "By all means, take a wheelchair with you at all times. Disney World is tiring for healthy people. Don't exacerbate your children's weariness by making them walk. The wheelchair and your GKTW button will also immediately identify you, so you won't have to wait in lines."

We received passes to all the attractions and were launched out on our own. In spite of sweltering temperatures, Kelly perked up considerably. I found it a little embarrassing to turn around occasionally and see her pushing Lauren or Leslie in the wheelchair, only to climb back into it when we appeared at the entrance to a specific ride. But within hours, we were grateful to have it for Kelly and didn't question further the need for it.

By the end of our first full day, all the exercise we got from walking had sufficiently unwound our anxiety. Gone were thoughts of terrorist attacks, illness, and death. We were settling in and beginning to relax on this wonderful gift vacation. Kelly, while tired, felt well, and for this we were grateful. She had no more headaches for the next several days, rode the thriller rides, and enjoyed eating and shopping for souvenirs.

Thursday night after supper, we returned to our villa to relax before bed. Suddenly Lauren shrieked. *"Dad! There's a monster spider in our room!"* Rob answered her urgent call. Sure enough, there was a thick black spider, the size of a small egg, making a lightning-fast beeline across the wall. I shivered to watch it; Rob yanked off his shoe for the kill, but it scampered sleekly out of sight—behind the built-in bookshelf. We pinned it captive with our gaze and dared it to come out. After 10 minutes of surveillance, we gave up.

"You're going to make us sleep in here, knowing that it's behind the bookshelf?" Leslie said, cringing.

"It's probably not going to go anywhere after all that exercise," Rob said. "I can't wait forever for it to come out."

The next afternoon, during a brief respite before dinner, the girls and I were watching TV and calmly looking through some of their souvenirs. Suddenly Lauren jumped off the sofa, sneaker in hand, and whacked the living daylights out of the spider, which had reappeared on the carpet in her line of vision. "I *GOT* him!" she said triumphantly. None of us knew whether any other Florida creatures lurked behind the furniture, but conquering what we did know about was comforting. We all breathed a sigh of relief and accompanied her to the bathroom to assure ourselves that the squashed carcass indeed got flushed down the toilet.

Saturday night we all decided to take an evening dip in the pool near our villa. Eagerly, Kelly swam—until I came up behind her and gently tried to hug her.

"Mom, ouch! That hurts!"

"What hurts?"

"Your touching my skin hurts."

"I hardly touched you, what do you mean?"

"It still hurt."

Bewildered by this, I let her swim alone. Later that night, my turn to tuck her in, I climbed into bed beside her. She snuggled close, her head with its slowly lengthening crop of now light brown hair nestled in the crook of my arm. I reached for Ted and perched him on top of my stomach.

"Tell me about your day," he said in his tiny treble voice, head cocking slightly to the side. "What did you do?"

"Well, we were at Universal Studios today and had lunch at the Hard Rock Cafe," Kelly said. "I wanted to stay longer, but Leslie didn't feel well."

"What did you have to eat?"

"A really big hamburger, chips, and a Coke."

"That sounds good. I had some crackers out of the refrigerator. What else did you see?" he said, hopping off my stomach and wedging himself between us, paws cupping his chin.

"We saw King Kong. That was really neat—and scary!"

"Oh, that sounds like so much fun!" We talked about some of the other events of the day; then Ted stretched his paws and yawned. "Oh, excuse me for yawning. It's just that—well, you were gone a really long time, and I was so busy myself today that I'm—well, *really* sleepy."

"Yeah, me, too."

"Why don't we say good-night to Mom, and then you and I can snuggle."

Kelly put her conversation with Ted on pause and turned a stiff, disappointed gaze onto me. "Mommy, don't make him say that."

"She's got laundry to do," Ted persisted, tapping her with his paw to get her attention. "Maybe she'll tickle our paws—oops, *arms*—before she goes."

"Okay," she sighed, stretching her bare arm over me.

A TABLE FOR TWO

After a few minutes of tickling, a brief prayer, and a kiss on her forehead, I got up and went to do the laundry. I didn't know then how much I'd later come to regret having let the immediacy of a chore come between me and my daughter's request for a little more of my presence.

Nobody told me this would be her last full night of earthly consciousness.

27.

Sunday morning, September 19th, the last day of our trip, dawned sunny and searingly hot. After breakfast we called Grandma to wish her a happy birthday. We knew she and Grandpa would be at church, so we prepared birthday greetings to leave on their answering machine. After a family prayer, we packed our things into the car, said good-bye to our wonderful villa, and headed off to Sea World.

The heat wilted all of us, but Kelly was unusually affected. "Do you feel okay?" I asked. She nodded that she was good enough. By late afternoon I was relieved to see her perk up. She giggled as she leaned over the dolphin pool and was able to snatch a fleeting feel of the soft wet skin of one of the friendly fish.

"Guys," Rob said, "unfortunately we've got to wrap this up. We've got to get to the airport soon." Everyone sighed with resignation; we were tired and hot and ready to find some air conditioning. A gift shop provided momentary relief while Kelly studied the seashell necklaces and purchased yet one more tangible memory of her trip.

It was 6:30 p.m. by the time we boarded the plane and got seated. Rob and Kelly got up to explore the cockpit, while Lauren and Leslie and I chatted about the trip and their adjustment to returning to school the next morning. I heard the fuzzy static of the intercom system come on and paused to hear what the pilots might have to say.

"Hi, Mom," came Kelly's voice over the plane, followed by a little giggle. By 7:00 the plane was airborne, and soon the flight attendants were moving through the aisles to hand out supper trays. Kelly, seated by Rob on the west side of the plane, ate ravenously and finished every last bite.

While we were eating, Rob tapped my shoulder. "Lis, look. Ever seen anything this pretty from 30,000 feet?" I turned to see an expansive, blazing red sunset over the deep horizon, poking through gray clouds like hot coals in the ashes of a fireplace. All of us sat mesmerized by the beauty until the last traces of light yielded to nightfall.

We landed at 9:30 p.m. in Baltimore, put on our jackets as we welcomed the fresh, crisp, fall air, and took a shuttle to the hotel where our van was parked. The girls were exhausted and quickly laid pillow claim to the back, middle, and reclining front seats. I sat in the middle seat with Kelly's legs over me, then, part way through the trip, moved to the floor to give her more space to sleep.

At 11:45 p.m. we pulled into our driveway and parked the car just outside the garage in order to allow space to unload. "Girls," Rob said, "we're home." Dutifully, Lauren and Leslie climbed out of their seats and went into the house to get ready for bed. Kelly didn't stir.

"Kelly, honey," I said, rubbing her legs. "We're home. Tucker's waiting for you." Rob scooped her out of the seat and carried her into the house where our dearly missed sheltie wriggled and squealed his greeting.

Kelly woke up immediately and dropped to her knees, embracing his neck and burying her nose in his fur. She smiled sleepily and said, "Oh, Sweetie . . . I missed you."

"Come on, Kelly, let's get you up to bed," Rob said. "Want me to carry you?" The two of them went upstairs with Tucker at their heels. I went out to the car to start unloading our things. After Rob got Kelly settled, he returned to help me. Within five minutes, however, we stopped in our tracks. Kelly was groaning loudly.

We raced upstairs. "What's the matter?" I said, her groaning getting louder.

"Kelly, be quiet!" came the voices of her sisters who were trying to sleep down the hall and assumed she was in one of her typically cranky states from having been awakened.

Suddenly Kelly sat up, clenched both sides of her head, and screamed at the top of her lungs, her eyes wide with panic, *"My head hurts!"*

I raced to get a basin and the medicine we'd been given, and then helped her swallow a quick dose. Within seconds, however, she vomited everything. She quieted down to a soft moan, and I could tell the intense pain was somewhat alleviated, but she continued to make bizarre thrashing motions with her arms and to pull at her waistband. I put my arms around her and held her close, trying to soothe her.

Finally she relaxed and let me lower her down into her pillow. Immediately, it seemed, she went to sleep.

Lauren and Leslie appeared in the doorway. "Is she okay?"

"I think so. Just a really bad headache this time. Go on. Everything's okay. Get some sleep now." I pulled the covers up to Kelly's chin, and Rob and I returned to the task of unpacking.

We collapsed into bed 20 minutes later, utterly spent. "I better check her one more time," I said, climbing back out of bed.

I leaned close to Kelly's face and heard a mild gagging sound from her throat. I immediately turned her on her side. "Do you need to vomit again?" I assumed her lack of response was due to the deep exhaustion we were all feeling. When all seemed to be well, her breathing peaceful and even, I kissed her forehead and returned to our room.

Rob and I lay silently beside each other. Dread and fear hung like shrouds over our bodies. "I feel like I should stay with her," I said.

"You'll hear her if she needs you," Rob assured me, taking my hand. "These could be long days ahead of us, and you'll need your sleep. We need to pray."

For a long time neither of us could speak about what felt so sore and swollen in our hearts. I could hear Rob crying softly, as I was, too. "Lord," he finally said. "If you have to take her, please . . . take her quickly. I can't bear to see her suffer."

During the night I heard a bump. I thought Tucker had rolled over and knocked the wall at the bottom of the steps where he sleeps, as he occasionally would do. I dismissed it and fell easily back into a deep sleep.

28.

"Lisa, wake up." Rob's words poked through the veil of my sleep. "I need you to help me. Kelly must have fallen out of bed last night. Let's move her in with you—I think she might have wet her bed a little."

I sat up, blearily eyeing the digital clock. It was 6:15 a.m. I followed him to her room, where, on the carpeted floor beside her bed, Kelly lay asleep on her back, legs stretched out.

"She's really chilly," I whispered, rubbing my hand across her bare legs, wishing we'd put more than a T-shirt on her the night before. Why hadn't I gotten up to check the noise I'd heard during the night? We had come, in a matter of hours, from sticky Florida weather in the mid-90's to the first invigorating coolness of our Pennsylvania fall. How long had she lain there? I guessed her level of exhaustion was too great for her to comprehend that she was uncovered.

Gingerly, so as not to disturb her, we lifted her off the floor and carried her back to our room. I crawled into bed beside her and gathered her close, anxious to warm her. Later I quietly slipped out of bed to help the other girls get ready for school.

"I can't believe she hasn't even stirred," I said to Rob as I came down the stairs. "I've never seen her this worn out."

Standing in front of the hallway mirror, Rob tugged at his

shirt collar and straightened his tie. "I could have used a few more hours of sleep myself."

"Me, too," I yawned, making my way into the kitchen.

"Mom, is Kelly going to school?" Leslie asked, zipping up her backpack.

"I don't know. Definitely not before lunchtime. Oh, Les, I need to write you and Lauren an excuse for last week." I fumbled in the desk drawer until I found the booklet of excuse slips. Tucker banged his nose against the wooden slats of the blinds on the back door. "Tuck, I'll let you out in a minute," I said, scratching a ballpoint pen across a tablet to get the ink started.

"Mom, is Kelly okay?" Lauren asked, coming into the kitchen.

"I don't know. I guess she's just exhausted. The trip was tiring for *us,* and *we're* healthy."

I handed the girls their excuses and let the dog out. Afterward, I went upstairs to check on Kelly. She had not changed positions. I touched her cheek with the back of my hand and tucked the covers closer around her neck. Her breathing was rhythmic, gentle, but not an arm or leg had shifted from the hour before.

"You know it's strange," I said to Rob when I returned downstairs. "She's so still it's almost like she's—in a coma or something."

"Is Kelly in a coma?" Lauren looked startled.

"I don't think so. But we'll have to wait and see how she does in the next couple of hours."

"Lauren, the bus is coming!" Leslie called from the living room.

"Bye," I said. "You guys have a good day."

"Mom, get Tucker inside—he's following us!" Tucker bounded back inside at my beckoning, slurped water from his bowl, then jerked his head out of the dish, scattering drops of water all over the floor. He scampered over to Rob, who stood at the counter laying sliced meat on a piece of sandwich bread.

Tucker sat at his feet, alert for any food to drop.

"Are you sure I should go to work?" Rob asked, ignoring the dog. "What if things aren't okay?"

"I'll call you if they're not. I'll let her sleep a while longer, and then see how she is."

"You don't think I should stay here?"

"No, it's okay. I'll call you either way in a couple of hours."

When he had gone, I went upstairs and put a load of clothes in the washer. Returning to our bedroom, I watched Kelly sleeping. Moving to the bed, I sat down beside her and studied her face. I recalled learning somewhere that people in comas had dilated pupils. After Kelly's surgery, the nurses checked her pupils regularly. Gently, I lifted her eyelids. Her pupils were enlarged and did not contract with the light. I went immediately to the phone.

"Is Dr. Close available, please?" I asked the oncology receptionist at Hershey Medical Center.

"I'm sorry, she's on vacation this week. Dr. Neely is on call, but he's in a meeting. Shall I have him call you when he's finished?"

"Yes, please." I hung up the phone, wondering what to do next. Then I quickly re-dialed the receptionist. "I should have told you the first time, but I think my daughter might be in a coma."

"Oh! I'll get him at once," she said, rapidly clicking me on hold. Within seconds, Dr. Neely, head of pediatric oncology, was on the phone. I had met him only one time before.

"I'm sorry," he said kindly. "Dr. Close is in Paris at the moment. What's happening with Kelly?"

He listened as I described her condition and named the medications she was taking, including the anti-seizure drug, Dylantin. "There is a possibility that the Dylantin has built up in her system, which could cause her to be comatose," he said. "The other possibility is that it's the tumors. If it's the Dylantin, she'll come out of it within a day, and we wouldn't treat her here with anything else." He paused, his voice gentle.

"It's my understanding that your wishes are not to prolong life with any further treatment, is that right?"

"Yes—just keep her comfortable."

"Then, either way, since she's comfortable, we wouldn't be doing anything for her here. All we could do for her is run a blood test and/or CAT scan to determine what's causing this. You and your husband need to decide whether that's something you'd like to have done. We'd be glad to have you come here, if you'd feel more comfortable knowing."

After hanging up with Dr. Neely, I called Rob, and we agreed that we didn't want to weather this alone, or uninformed. Within 30 minutes we had Kelly wrapped in blankets, stretched out in the back of the van, and were on our way to Hershey. Arriving at the hospital 40 minutes later, we were immediately ushered into a room where we laid her on an examining table. A nurse checked her, then closed the door and left us alone to wait for Dr. Neely.

Rob pulled up a stool beside Kelly, put his right arm across her waist, and with his left hand, sat stroking her head. He tenderly smoothed the new, small growth of bangs off to the side of her forehead and kissed her. Then he touched his own forehead to hers. "Kelly," he whispered in her ear, his chin quivering slightly, "it's all right with us if—"

His voice caught in his throat. Locating her hand under the blanket, he squeezed it. "— if Jesus wants you to come to heaven." Lifting his head, his face heavy with sorrow, he wiped a tear, then placed his hand back on her head and lovingly stroked her hair. "We'll catch up to you later—as soon as we can."

Dr. Neely entered the room and shook hands with each of us. "I'm so sorry Dr. Close is unable to be here with you." He moved to Kelly's side. "You've tried to wake her up?"

"Well, not exactly," I said. "But she would have awakened from all the times we moved her this morning, don't you think?"

"Yes, I'm sure." He studied her chart for a moment, then closed it. "I didn't realize she's only been on Dylantin for three weeks. The small dosage she's on wouldn't be enough to cause this." He paused and studied her carefully. "I'm going to summon a neurologist. Excuse me for a moment, will you?"

A few minutes later he returned with a teenaged girl. "This is Diane," he said softly, "and she's going to stay with Kelly while we talk in another room." He turned to the girl. "Diane, this is Kelly, and she's having a really good sleep. Will you stay with her and call us if she wakes up?" Diane nodded cheerfully and sat on the stool Rob had occupied.

Out in the hall I looked at Dr. Neely curiously. "I didn't want to upset her," he said. "She's a new volunteer." We walked with him into a conference room where the neurologist greeted us and informed us that he was a close friend of Dr. Janss's in Philadelphia.

He motioned for us to sit down. "I've looked at Kelly's MRI scans from last month, and the only way to tell what's going on now is to give her a CAT scan. It would only take a few minutes. It's up to you—whatever you'd like."

I looked at Rob, trying to read his face. "I guess I would like to know," I said. "It feels better knowing what's going on for sure." Rob nodded in agreement, and the doctor went to call to set up the appointment.

We returned to the examining room where Diane was reading a book beside Kelly. "She did fine," she said. "She didn't stir at all."

"Thanks," I said.

Within minutes the nurses brought a gurney, and both doctors escorted us to the waiting area for the scan. We stood for nearly a half hour, chatting easily with them. "This is pretty incredible," I said, rubbing Kelly's feet to try to bring warmth into her body, "having the head of pediatric oncology and a neurologist escort us and stay with us for all this time. Thanks."

"No problem," Dr. Neely said, offering a sympathetic smile.

"We can go in now," the other doctor said, taking the head of the gurney and pulling it away from the wall. He looked at us. "I'm sorry, you'll need to stay here in the waiting area."

"One more thing," Dr. Neely said slowly. "The technicians in there are all set up to go to any lengths, should a patient stop breathing. Am I correct that you wish to have no life-support-ive measures taken, if this happens?"

We nodded silently, and the two men wheeled Kelly through the doors into the scanning area. Within 10 minutes they returned. Dr. Neely's face was all seriousness. He moved toward us and motioned us a distance away. "Things have taken a very serious turn. She is hemorrhaging massively, and it looks as if the tumors have mushroomed in size since her last scan." He paused to allow us to absorb the information. "Normally, it takes 24-48 hours for a coma to deepen. There are rare patients who pull through something like this, but I . . . think it highly unlikely in her case. We could admit her, if you'd like."

"No," Rob said slowly, lowering his head and taking a deep breath. "Her wish was to be at home."

The neurologist put his hand on Rob's shoulder. "I'll call Dr. Janss and let her know what's going on." I took my place at Kelly's side while the two men escorted us back to the oncolo-gy clinic. "I'll need to be going," he said gently. "I'm very sorry you couldn't be with your regular doctors today."

We were moved by their mercy, ministered to by their will-ingness to be present with us for over two hours. While Rob left to bring the car up to the entrance, Dr. Neely and I talked quietly. "Is there anything we should do to care for her?" I asked. "Should we call hospice or a visiting nurse?"

"If you would feel more secure," he said, volunteering to make the necessary calls. Then he grew quiet, his eyes focused on Kelly. I looked anxiously into his face. "For a moment there," he said, "I thought she had stopped breathing."

I looked closely at Kelly and was relieved to see the gentle heave of her chest resume. "How long do you think she has?"

"It's hard to tell. A day or two possibly." He paused, speak-ing gently. "It's not always easy to tell when death happens. Sometimes it will be 15 or 20 minutes before you know for sure."

Rob came in the building and scooped Kelly into his arms. "Thank you, Dr. Neely," I said. "We're really grateful for everything."

"Please call me if anything changes."

"We will," I said, taking his outstretched hand. "Good-bye."

When we arrived back home, we laid Kelly on the family-room sofa. I had been trying all day, to no avail, to warm her body. Finally I took her warmest winter hat, a soft cream-colored one with a thick wreath of silky white fur around the crown, and tied it beneath her chin. She looked serene, beautiful, like a fairy-tale snow princess.

It was 2:15 p.m. Rob and I agreed it would be better to pick up each of the girls at school, rather than have them get off the bus and be shocked to find Kelly in her present condition. With him gone, I sat on the floor beside Kelly and reached under the blankets to hold her hand. Tucker nestled against the sofa, as he always did when she lay there watching TV.

I pressed my lips and nose into her cheek, trying desperately to find and hold onto her in this sickly still state. I didn't know how to act—quiet and respectful of one sleeping? Careful what I say? Talk or not talk to her? Dr. Neely had said there's a possibility she could hear us. From the moment I had changed, washed, and dressed her limp body before we left for the hospital, Kelly seemed gone to me. It was hard to talk to her when she didn't even seem present. I found myself thinking how I'd get fluids into her, what I might feed her to sustain her. I found it exceedingly difficult to accept that she simply would not be eating or drinking anymore.

I knelt next to her and began to softly sing the hymn that had sustained me before her radiation treatments: *Other refuge have I none, hangs my helpless soul on thee; leave, ah! leave me not alone, still support and comfort me. All my trust on thee is stayed, all my help from thee I bring; cover my defenseless head with the shadow of thy wing. . .*

I closed my eyes as I lay my head beside hers. Memories from the year before echoed gently in my mind. I saw us walking hand-in-hand down to the neighborhood store three weeks after her surgery. *Mommy, could I die from this? . . . I'm not afraid to die, because I know I'll be with Jesus. I'm just afraid of how I would die . . .*

I had choked back a tidal wave of emotion and tried to answer the question as helpfully as possible: *Probably we would be holding you, and it would be just like we passed you right into the arms of Jesus . . .*

A month later, at the Ronald McDonald House in Philadelphia, she had stumbled upon a pamphlet. *What does thirty-percent 'sur-vivval' rate mean?* she had asked. Moments later, lying on the bed in our room, Kelly cradled under my arm beside me, we had come to terms with each of our imminent deaths and had begun to giggle about the imagined joys of heaven. Her eyes had lit up with expectation: *O Mommy, I want to go to heaven right now!*

So do I, I had answered in one heartfelt cry to escape all the tribulation of the illness. *Hey, why don't we jump onto the trauma helicopter and go right now?*

The idea amused us both, as we had watched the helicopter land on the roof outside our seventh floor hospital room numerous times. We laughed in the warm shadow of God's wing. Now I felt the coolness not just of her body, but of the valley of the shadow of death.

The sound of the doorbell broke into my reverie. Ma-Ma and Pop-Pop had arrived with the items I asked them to pick up. I quickly alerted them to her now confirmed state, and they went, painfully, to her side. It had been their deepest desire to take Kelly to Disney World, and now she couldn't even tell them about her trip. It seemed strange for me to try to do it for her. Instead, I reached over to the table and picked up a small bag. "Here," I said, handing it to my mother-in-law. "Yesterday Kelly saw this in a store at Sea World and asked if she could buy it for you. She said it reminded her of you." Ma-Ma carefully opened the bag and pulled out a necklace of tiny pink, white, and coral-colored shells. "I'm sorry, the fastener is broken. We didn't know it when we—"

My voice trailed off as I saw her face fill with pain. Struggling to clench back her tears, she tightened her lip. "Kelly, thank you. . . . This is the most beautiful gift."

Pop-Pop stood watching from the corner of the sofa, then turned and removed his glasses to wipe the tears from his eyes.

The phone rang. Answering it, I was grateful to hear the voice of Pastor David. He started to ask about our trip, but I interrupted him. "David, Kelly's in a coma," I said, giving way to deep sobs. I blurted out the rest of the story as best as I could.

"Keep talking to her," he said gently. "She probably hears you."

After I hung up the phone, Ma-Ma and Pop-Pop said they would leave and come back later, allowing the rest of the family, who had just come in the door, to be alone with Kelly for a while.

Lauren and Leslie, briefed by Rob on the way home, set down their backpacks and gathered around Kelly. Tucker moaned eagerly for their attention, but their eyes stayed focused on their sister. We talked quietly for a few moments, and then the doorbell rang again. I opened the door to find our dear neighbors, the Oberts, standing on the sidewalk, smiling.

"Welcome home!" they cheered happily. "We just wanted to come by and hear about your trip!"

"Is Kelly inside?" 10-year-old Lisa asked eagerly, looking past me into the hallway.

"Wait—" I said, putting my hand on her shoulder and blocking her from entering. Lisa looked up into my face, startled. "We've had an unfortunate turn of events." The joy immediately left their faces. "You can come in, Lisa, but you need to know something first. Kelly's in what's called a 'coma,' and that means that she looks like she's sleeping, but she won't be able to talk to you."

Lisa's mother, Sally, burst into tears.

"We had a wonderful trip," I continued, putting my arms around her. "But last night, right after we got home, she had a violent headache, and then apparently slipped into a coma, which we discovered this morning." I looked at Lisa's bewildered face. I tried to lighten the mood. "Lisa, wait 'til you see what Kelly bought you! If you want to come in and see her, I'll get it for you."

She nodded, and I led her and Sally into the family room. Reaching into a small bag, I pulled out a gold Mickey Mouse pin, outlined in tiny gold studs. Lisa's face brightened. "She picked it out just for you," I said.

Lisa looked at her dear friend and said, "Kelly, thank you so much!" At that moment, Kelly's breathing rattled audibly. "Mom!" Lisa cried triumphantly. "She heard me! I know she heard me!"

While they stayed with Kelly a few more moments, I went to answer another phone call. When I came back, I noticed that Kelly's lips had taken on a purplish color. "Lisa, we need to let this family alone now," her mother said. "We'll come back tomorrow."

When they had gone, Rob answered another phone call, this time from Pastor Tom. Lauren, Leslie, and I gathered around Kelly. I knelt near her face, noticing the color deepening in her lips. Holding her hand and stroking her shoulder, I fixed my gaze on her. After several moments I asked them, "Have either of you seen her breathe?" We all quieted, trying to perceive the slightest movement from her chest. "I don't think she's taken a breath in the last few minutes."

I pressed my ear to her heart. Hearing nothing, I waited another moment. "Rob," I called.

"Tom, hold on a minute," he said.

"I think. . . I think she's gone," I said, laying my head on her chest and letting my tears spill upon her blanket. I slid my arm under her neck and drew her close, my heart throbbing against her lifeless body. Rob and the girls had melted themselves on top of us, and I drew away, giving them a chance to hold her. Together we knelt beside her, our bodies pressed against one another to absorb and distribute the deepening sorrow.

Pastors, family, friends, a policeman, and a doctor all came through our house in the ensuing hours. We even ate supper with Kelly still lying just a few feet away. It felt familiar, comforting—like all the times she lay there when she didn't feel well enough to join us for a meal.

Four-and-a-half hours after her death, we sat across the kitchen table from the undertaker, who recorded information for the obituary and patiently helped us work out plans for the funeral. Pastor David had also come to be with us, offering comforting and thorough counsel.

When we finished, I went over to the sofa for one last look before they took her body away. The funeral directors suggested that we might want to leave the room, but all of us, including the children, opted to stay. We watched mournfully as they carried her outside.

When David had gone, the four of us stood silently in the kitchen, stunned by the absence which was so heavily upon us. The sofa, with blankets in fresh disarray from her body being pulled from them, seemed to radiate an ethereal energy. She was gone, but where to? She had made the transition from this life to the next, and the mystery of it all—of life slipped out of the shell of visible form—stirred eerily among us. The girls felt it, too, and as we turned off the lights in the family room before going to bed, they clung close and begged us to sleep with them, which we did on Lauren's bedroom floor, since our bed had been badly soiled.

We lay in the darkness of her room, staring at the glowing stars pasted on her ceiling. "Just think," Rob said. "Yesterday afternoon Kelly was petting dolphins at Sea World.

"Twenty-four hours later, she's gone from life on this earth. It's almost like she stepped right from the Magic Kingdom into God's Heavenly Kingdom."

We talked of the flaming red sunset she had seen at 30,000 feet from the airplane, of the meal she had eaten so voraciously, of her talking to me over the pilot's intercom. Then Lauren's voice came, timidly, from the bed above us. "Dad, I'm afraid."

"Afraid of what?"

"That Kelly will appear to me—and scare me."

"Scare you?"

"Yes," Leslie said. "Kelly was teasing us a few weeks ago and said that after she dies she's going to sneak around and go 'boo' when we least expect it. Will she be able to do something like that?"

The feisty younger sister had called upon her mischievous prowess and found an upbeat, creative way to overcome the gloom of her poor prognosis. A chuckle rose up in the room, foiling the fear, lightening the pain.

29.

The late afternoon sun lay in a soft amber wash over the northwest section of the cemetery. Rob and I got out of our car and walked to the place where, the day before, we had gathered around Kelly's white, youth-sized casket and bid our final farewell to the part of her we knew in a physical sense—where love and faith, mischief and pain played the symphony of life, and summoned, with their intricate melodies and rhythms, her face, her hands, her being. The last movement, the grand finale of pain, had swept its dissonant chords and turbulent rhythms all through her, and, in one violent cymbal crash, she had clutched her head in her hands and surrendered to its final fermata.

Holding each other, we stood in silence over the colorful spray of casket flowers which lay in a delicate heap on the mound of freshly turned earth. There is no rightness in such a moment, and there is no peace. Obsessed with retrieving her from this cruel encasement, my body shook with the desire to unearth her, to dig furiously like a dog to bring her back, to pound the unrelenting sod and scream in loud, throbbing echoes my dissenting voice to this entire ordeal.

We had touched her body for the last time the morning of the burial. I had pressed my cheek to hers, kissed her forehead, held her hand, wept profusely with the others. Because I needed to know, I had stood for a moment behind her head—the vantage point in my vision of her when she was a year old, lying dead as an older child in a white bed—and saw it nearly exactly as I had then. And there they were: the puzzling, white, bar-like lines were the sun rays shooting out in a pleated semicircle of spokes from the sunrise sewn into the white satin interior of the lid. There was no space within my heart to do more than numbly ponder it all. Should I have been comforted by the vision when it occurred—or now? Should I have found solace in what must have been God's foreknowledge and preparation, God, as intimate friend, letting me in—albeit mysteriously—on his agenda? Yes—and no.

There were few vacant spaces to be found in the parking lot of the church that evening at the memorial service. An usher motioned us to a far area—then, realizing who we were, looked horrified at his mistake and apologetically gestured us to a spot near the door. We went inside and met the funeral director and other members of our family in the nursery.

In the hallway, on a special table, were all the things we could collect that symbolized Kelly: trinkets from Disney World, her pencil collection, her Bible, favorite books, her special handmade necklaces and—in the center—the enlarged photographs that Lauren had taken of her only two months before. It was for this night, I surmised, that I had unknowingly held them in my heart. Propped up beside the display board was Teddy—whom we had asked the funeral director to remove from Kelly's casket prior to its final closing.

Two nights before, the church had been equally crowded as friends and family came to view Kelly's body. Tonight, the memorial service would be the final, culminating event. I was grateful we had stretched the ceremony into three separate days.

I leaned close to the speaker mounted on the wall of the nursery to try to hear the prelude music our dear friends from our concert group, On Bended Knee, had planned and organized for this night. We made some suggestions to them but felt confidence, as well as relief, in letting them plan the rest. Rob nudged me and gestured toward the wall where a large quilt hung. Our eyes filled as we read the words appliqued on it: *That's Our Baby.*

"If you'll please follow me now," the funeral director said, "I think we're ready to begin." He ushered us down the hall and through the makeshift aisle among the people in the overflow section in the fellowship hall. As we entered the sanctuary I melted when I heard the strains of my own choral arrangement of *In Thee is Gladness,* played joyfully and exquisitely on the piano, flute, two violins, and two cellos. I smiled at this heavenly surprise, and immediately thought of our first day at CHOP when that song came to my mind in the lobby of the hospital. Our friends, plumbing the pain, as well as finding the faith of our hearts, were letting us know through their instruments that they were walking this journey with us.

We looked around at all the people from On Bended Knee who had come to lend their support and worship to our evening. Soon the brass, flute, strings, and voices swelled like a tidal wave of hope with the organ and congregation as the strains of *Joyful, Joyful, We Adore Thee* filled the church. The words, powerfully magnified by nearly a thousand tongues, came like strong supporting arms underneath us: *Melt the clouds of sin and sadness, drive the dark of doubt away; Giver of immortal gladness, fill us with the light of day.*

Pastor Tom opened Kelly's lavender-colored Bible and read from Psalm 23: "You prepare a table before me in the presence of my enemies," he said, pausing to look out over the people. "Kelly's enemy was cancer, and Christ showed her, in a dream state, the table he had prepared for her."

The pianist played the opening strains of *I Am the Bread of Life* while Lauren and Leslie got up from their seats and went to the altar area under the cross where we had set up a small communion table with two chairs. While Pastor David sang the song, Leslie unfolded a royal purple tablecloth a friend had made especially for us and laid it over the table. Lauren set it with two white plates which—surprisingly, as they had come from my mother and Kelly had never seen them—had a raised grapevine pattern on the rims, similar to Kelly's dream description. In the center, Leslie placed a clear, glass, tapered candlestick, also belonging to my mother and which fit Kelly's dream specifications. Lauren and Leslie lit the candle, then sat down while Pastor David finished the song: . . . *And I will raise him up, and I will raise him up, and I will raise him up on the last day.*

Pastor Tom stood to deliver the meditation. ". . . God tells us in his Word that he spoke and will continue to speak through dreams," he said. "And I believe God is telling us to find special hope in this dream." He turned to the back of the bulletin where we had printed my brief description of the dream and continued: "Kelly's mother asked her how she knew it was Jesus who was eating with her, and Kelly said, 'I just *knew.*' After the resurrection seven disciples were by the Sea of Galilee, and when Peter said he was going fishing, the rest joined him. They caught nothing. Then Jesus, standing on the shore, told them to cast to the other side, and, when they did, they hauled in a great catch. John says they were afraid to ask him, 'Are you Jesus?' But they *just knew.* Jesus says, 'My sheep know me, and they listen to my voice, and I give them eternal life. They shall never perish, and no one can snatch them out of my hand.'

". . . Eating has always been symbolic in Scripture to represent fellowship with God. What a beautiful way to comprehend the tender intimacy with Christ at the great marriage feast of the multitudes in heaven—to think of eating alone with him at a table for two. Kelly said there was no food present. Jesus told his disciples, 'I have food to eat that you know nothing about. My food is to do the will of the Father . . . .'"

In the receiving line after the service, a five-year-old boy pressed a card into my hand. On it was a simple sketch he had drawn of two people eating at a table together. "Kelly and

Jesus," he had written on the bottom. Another little girl from our neighborhood, who had attended the viewing and seen the memorial table in the hallway, clutched her own stuffed lovie and wondered why we had taken Kelly's teddy out of her casket. Still another wrote a letter saying she was happy Kelly could finally see Elvis.

It was the children who continued to be of concern to me in the coming weeks as we worked through the raw stages of inchoate grief. Although glad that their parents hadn't shielded them from the experience of death, I wondered how they were handling it and whether they had questions they couldn't articulate. I was drawn to them, both to comfort them and to be comforted by them.

A month after the funeral I took a vacation video to school for the children of Kelly's class. The last clip I showed was Kelly smiling and waving good-bye to Sea World from her wheelchair. "Good-bye," she said, giggling. It was a fitting closure for her fellow students, who had never gotten a chance to say farewell or to hear her tell about her trip.

We were deeply touched by Mrs. Charles's willingness to freely address loss and grief issues with her third-grade students. They adopted a whale in Kelly's name, and they wrote their feelings down in letters to her, which they then collected and mounted in a scrapbook for us. One young classmate visited our home with her mother a few days later and wanted me to recount every minute detail of Kelly's death, including on which of our two sofas the death actually occurred and how Kelly's head was turned, since she'd heard that a bit of saliva had rolled down Kelly's chin. I didn't question how she got this information; I was just gratcful for her and all the other children's straightforward interest. I relished being able to talk with many of them, welcomed all their questions, cherished their embraces, and encouraged them to stop by and jump on the trampoline.

Gradually, as children convinced their parents that it was okay in spite of the circumstances, and that we really wanted them to come jump on the trampoline, the backyard again buzzed with activity. Like messengers of healing, the kids did what only a few adults felt free to do—they talked to us about Kelly, asked if they could have something of hers to keep, hung around the kitchen just to be with us.

The doorbell rang one late afternoon just before supper. "Mrs. Bair," said the little girl staring up at me and smiling shyly. "My friends said we were allowed to have something of Kelly's."

I took her hand, led her upstairs, and opened Kelly's closet, pulling down three stuffed animals. "Which one do you like the best?" I asked. She chose a soft brown puppy, smiled, and hugged me hard as she pressed him to her face.

The children kept us entering Kelly's room and helped to prevent the flow of her life from getting clogged in our grief-swollen hearts. "Don't avoid going into the house of memories," Pastor David had told me before Kelly died. The children seemed to understand this instinctively.

There wasn't a place in our home that exclusively embodied the memory of Kelly more than her bedroom. Many nights, upon closing my eyes to try and sleep, I couldn't erase the images of Kelly's violent headache. It pierced my heart that I had hugged her that night only to quiet her, not as a mother saying good-bye in her child's last moments of earthly consciousness. The scene replayed in torturous proportions until I would either sob myself helplessly to sleep or open my eyes to try and diffuse the intensity. One particularly bad night I climbed out of bed and went to Kelly's room, pulled back the covers of her bed and found, by sleeping in it, the first real solace and relief to these grueling episodes.

Another night, desperate for a connection with her, I pleaded with God to let me dream of Kelly. While in fact she did appear in my dream that night—standing on a chair at the kitchen sink refilling Tucker's water dish and telling me she was fine—Lauren also dreamed of her that same night, and I found far more comfort and intrigue in hers.

"Mom," Lauren told me the next morning, "I dreamed I was writing at my desk, and I turned around and was startled to see Kelly lying on my bed drawing pictures like she would sometimes do. I asked her how she got here, and she said, 'I was allowed to come visit.' Then she looked at me, smiled, and said, 'Lauren, you'll really love heaven when you get there!' I asked her to tell me about it and she said she wasn't allowed to, but she did say, 'Today we were playing in the wheat.' Then she said she had to go, and I pleaded for her not to, but she smiled and told me again how much I'd love heaven. Then she got in a white van that had flowers on the sides, and she was driven away." Lauren's face clouded, and her dark eyes filled with tears. "I didn't want her to go."

For six straight weeks Tucker bounded to the window at the sound of Kelly's school bus and squealed in anticipation of her. When she didn't come, he'd retrace with his eyes the path from the bus all the way to our front door and back again. Puzzled, he'd finally lie down when the bus drove off, leaving me once more in an emotionally wrenched state.

Tucker wasn't the only one searching for Kelly to come home. Many nights, it seemed, one or another of us would need to lie down on the living room sofa in the dark for a while before coming to bed—lamenting yet another day with no sign of her. The teddy bear had become for all of us the closest link to her. Permanently stationed on the sofa, he absorbed many tears, and, if walls could speak, they'd tell you a tiny, cartoon voice did an awfully lot of counseling and healing.

30.

The size two brown suede boots minus the fancy nylon ties stood neatly at attention in front of the white bureau. I couldn't remember the boots having been moved or even touched since Kelly put them there when she returned from camp. The boots worn for only a week. The boots I hadn't wanted her to buy because they seemed too frivolously elegant for camp life. The boots Rob had told her to save for school and not to ruin at camp. Now, only slightly broken in and minimally soiled, they were the boots with no regrets—symbols on the feet of a little girl whose life merited, in its melancholy, a dash of élan. I stood in the doorway of Kelly's bedroom, looking at them fairly simmering in their silence with the memory of the warm and winsome feet that slipped joyfully in and out of them.

Several times daily, for months after she died, I had gone into her bedroom to soak in the poetic stillness of her personal effects—and to cry. Often the tears would be triggered by something that seemed to have nothing to do with grief. Slowly I began to absorb the fact that *everything* in my life had to do with it, and—like a rushing river in my soul pressing against the walls of a great dam—grief spilled into every conceivable opening. Often its surging velocity crashed through the walls of routine living which could, only feebly, hold it at bay. Helpless and floundering in all its turbulence, I wordlessly cursed its unpredictable flow, spit out sand, and nursed my abrasions when I felt slapped to the beach and washed up like weathered debris.

In the middle of it all, though largely imperceptible to us at the time, we were being helped and moved along by the rough rapids of grief's perplexing course. To surrender to its precarious navigation was, in retrospect, the only path to healing. Many people who had talked freely of Kelly's illness while she was alive were now strangely silent. I learned in time that they feared "stirring us up." Little did they know how necessary and healing the stirring can be, and how the river of grief churns constantly anyway. No friend or acquaintance can possibly stir up what has become, for the newly bereaved, the voluminous preoccupation of their souls.

We learned to accept the fact that the journey of grief could not be carefully calculated—only submitted to. In time we gave ourselves the permission to avoid sewing up neat answers for others who asked about how we were doing. We tried to let the myth unravel that we were "strong and full of faith." We discovered that the appearance of strength carries with it an element of loneliness; did we need to completely lose composure in public for the great cry of our souls to be acknowledged? What did I really want from people anyway? As I pondered this desperate expectation of people and my corresponding disappointment, I concluded only one thing: I wanted someone to give my daughter back.

The morning Rob and I decided we would clean her bedroom and sort through her things, Kelly's boots were like everything else in her room—mute contrasts to the loud, clashing internal upheaval that characterized our hearts. Today we would move the boots and stir all of her belongings from their death-sacred paralysis. Something in us knew it was time—time to redefine the room's use for our family, to acknowledge that life had stopped in it, and to begin deliberately living and moving in it.

A TABLE FOR TWO

It is the smallest but sunniest bedroom in our house, and the white walls and furniture bounced the light that morning to the point of glare. I sat down on Kelly's bed and scanned the shelves of her beloved books, toys, and stuffed animals glistening in the sun. I moved to her dresser and gingerly began to empty her clothes from it. Rob began pulling books off the shelf.

Tenderly, I sorted through the T-shirts, nighties, pants, sweaters—many of which had not been worn much or at all. I came upon several new sweater and pants sets for winter which Kelly had received as "early Christmas presents." No one dared say that they weren't expecting Kelly to live until Christmas; no one wanted to do anything but celebrate the moment, at whatever the cost or impracticality. I thought of some of Kelly's young friends. They would grow nicely into these clothes. Would they feel comfortable wearing them? Could I bear to see them in her clothes?

I moved to the closet and pulled her dresses off the hangers. What was in good condition filled a big box almost entirely. But in my hand I held the baby blue denim jumper and white cotton T-shirt Lauren had photographed Kelly in two months before her death. These I could not part with. They felt limp and tender with the absence of her body, like soft gloves pulled from the warm fingers of a young child. I pressed my face into them and tried to discern her scent, held them up to myself and hugged them like she was in them.

Rob had his own moments of tears, too, as Winnie the Pooh and Dr. Seuss books made their way into boxes, bringing back countless nights of lying together reading on her bed. At what age had we stopped reading to her? When did she begin reading to us? Homemade stories of Fred, the Bug-in-the-Rug, and The Jelly Bean Antics rang out in the room. It was tender and too much. Tears flowing, we stopped to feel the bittersweetness—Rob now sitting on the floor with his head leaning back on the wall, and me curled up on the bed with my head on her pillow.

It was emotionally exhausting work and took us almost the entire day. Finally, the room vacuumed and stripped sterile, we looked forlornly at one another. I turned longingly to the only remaining evidence of the fun-loving youngster that once inhabited the room—the red crayon marks I had once scolded Kelly for scribbling on the white lampshade on her bedside table.

The bedside table. My eyes fell to the single drawer just below the lamp. We'd forgotten all about it. Opening it, I discovered treasures, six inches deep—trinkets, markers, barrettes, memo pads, small plastic toys, and rubber, animal-shaped erasers. Souvenirs of a young life. The stuff of being a child. I sorted through it all, then lifted out what lay at the very bottom—a large black-and-white-marbled composition notebook. Tenderly I opened it, hoping to see a drawing, spelling words, *anything.* I let the book's pages slide slowly away from my thumb as I perused blank page after blank page. Then my heart stopped to see more than I had wished for. Some writing. *Journal entries.* I summoned Rob, who was in the hall organizing the boxes and bags. He sat down beside me on the bed and together we wept with gratitude, reading what felt like a personal letter to us from Kelly in her new residence—a heavenly benediction our hearts desperately needed:

Dear Jesus,

I really felt much closer to you these past years, and I still do. I have felt your presents more. I thank you for this time of cancer through the past year and a-half. It has given me a time to get even closer to you! I am so excited to come to your kingdom someday! I don't know anything about what heaven looks like, I

> Know it's going to be the best place I have ever been! I can't wait! It feels so good to know that I'm in your arms, safe and sound! I love you so much I can't explain how much! I couldn't of goten through last year without you Jesus!!! This year I really feel like one of God's mitionaris. I feel a mesag to tell people about God! It's a very, very, very neat and special feeling!

The entries were dated early July 1993—a week or so after Kelly's dream of eating with Jesus at their table for two. Reading these words, I was filled with intense longing to know more fully the beauty of the holiness she saw and tasted—that caused her to rejoice in the midst of her illness, bask in the joyful intimacy of friendship with God, and want to reach out with the good news of redemptive hope. I thought of the note a little girl handed to us after Kelly's memorial service: "Dear Kelly," she wrote. "Enjoy your supper with God. Love, Brittany Riegen."

Supper with God. It brought to mind the words of Christ: *Here I am! I stand at the door and knock. If anyone hears my voice and opens the door, I will come in and eat with him, and he with me.*

The aroma of the Bread of Life drifted from the kitchen of the kingdom of God. My host seemed to stand before me, holding out the chair opposite his own, offering himself for all of time.

To him who overcomes,
I will give some of the hidden manna . . .
                                        —Revelation 2:17

"Kelly's Dream"

It was early on a summer morning back in June of '93
And the birds were singin' gloriously while I was sipping tea
At the kitchen table, hopin' for another quiet hour
Before the kids would be arisin', and I'd have to get my shower.

A gentle breeze floated through the open windowsill;
I closed my eyes and drank in smells from honeysuckle hills.
Then way before I wanted to, I heard the top step creak,
And down the stairs came padding feet; I turned around to peek.

I was surprised to see her first, my youngest of the three,
The latest sleeper of the bunch,
"Darlin', what're you doin' up so early?"

She came to me and touched my arm, looked deep into my eyes,
Her face was soft and tender like the newborn light of sunrise. . . .

"Mommy, I had the best dream! I dreamed I was with Jesus.
"Mommy, we were eating, but I don't remember any food,
"Oh, I feel so close to God. . . ."

I saw within her gentle smile the absence of all pain.
I asked her how she knew it was he;
she looked wistful, then explained:

"I just knew! I just knew! We were eating at a table for two.
"I just knew! I just knew! We were eating at a table for two . . ."

A TABLE FOR TWO

Three months later Jesus called the maître d' of heaven;
"Reservations, please," he said,
"for a little girl one year past seven."
Then reaching at the appointed time to lift her from her bed,
He drew her from the bonds of earth to feast on Living Bread.

Come, dine at the table for two.
The dream was for her, but it's also for you.
Come and drink deeply of all that Christ is,
And open your heart to the life that he gives.

Come, dine at the table for two.
Eat as your bread words that are true.
Come and drink deeply of all that Christ is,
And open your heart to the life that he gives.
Open your heart to the life that he gives.

—words & music by Alisa Bair
© June 1995

Sources

Pages 33, 201

Lindemann, Johann. "In Thee Is Gladness." Translation by Catherine Winkworth, 1858. Music by Giovanni Giacomo Gastoldi, 1593. SATB arrangement with optional flute and handbells by Alisa Bair. Miami, FL. Belwin Mills, 1992.

Page 43

Watterson, Bill. *The Indispensable Calvin and Hobbes.* Kansas City, MO: Andrews and McMeel, 1992.

Pages 47, 48

Engelmann, Kim. "Sudden Fury." *Guideposts,* Vol. 46, No. 8 (1991).

Page 61

Driskell, Gary. "Another Time, Another Place." Irving, TX: Word Music, 1990.

Pages 72, 193

Wesley, Charles. "Jesus, Lover of My Soul." Music by Joseph Parry, 1879.

About the Author

Alisa Bair is a musician and published composer.

Trained in music therapy and music education at East Carolina University in Greenville, North Carolina, Alisa is currently minister of music and worship at her church. She lives in Lancaster, Pennsylvania, with her husband and two daughters.

Her writings have been published in *Guideposts*.